# GROWING STRONG

## IN GOD'S FAMILY

This book belongs to: _____

# GROWING STRONG
## IN GOD'S FAMILY

A COURSE IN PERSONAL DISCIPLESHIP TO STRENGTHEN YOUR WALK WITH GOD

THE 2:7 SERIES

1

NAVPRESS

*A NavPress resource published in alliance
with Tyndale House Publishers, Inc.*

NCM

NAVIGATOR CHURCH MINISTRIES

NavPress is the publishing ministry of The Navigators, an international Christian organization and leader in personal spiritual development. NavPress is committed to helping people grow spiritually and enjoy lives of meaning and hope through personal and group resources that are biblically rooted, culturally relevant, and highly practical.

**For more information, visit www.NavPress.com.**

*Growing Strong in God's Family: A Course in Personal Discipleship to Strengthen Your Walk with God*

Copyright © 2011 by The Navigators. All rights reserved.

A NavPress resource published in alliance with Tyndale House Publishers, Inc.

ISBN 978-1-61521-639-0

Printed in the United States of America

21 20 19 18 17 16 15
14 13 12 11 10 9  8

## ACKNOWLEDGMENT

We are grateful for the dedicated efforts of Ron Oertli, who originated the concept of THE 2:7 SERIES and is its principal author. Ron is also the key person responsible for this updated edition. This discipleship training approach began in Denver in 1970 and continues to be highly effective in many places around the world.

# CONTENTS

# MY COMPLETION RECORD

As you complete each item, ask someone in your group to sign off for that item with his or her initials and the calendar date.

| SCRIPTURE MEMORY | INITIALS | DATE |
|---|---|---|
| *Beginning with Christ* (*BWC*) memory verses: | | |
| "Assurance of Salvation" (1 John 5:11-12) | | |
| "Assurance of Answered Prayer" (John 16:24) | | |
| "Assurance of Victory" (1 Corinthians 10:13) | | |
| "Assurance of Forgiveness" (1 John 1:9) | | |
| "Assurance of Guidance" (Proverbs 3:5-6) | | |
| Optional outreach verse (John 5:24) | | |
| Quoted all *BWC* verses at one sitting | | |
| Reviewed all *BWC* verses for 7 consecutive days | | |
| **QUIET TIME** | | |
| Completed *My Reading Highlights* for 7 consecutive days | | |
| **BIBLE STUDY** | | |
| Session 2—*Beginning with Christ Bible Study* (pages 28–32) | | |
| Session 3—Prayer: Part 1 (pages 40–42) | | |
| Session 4—Prayer: Part 2 (pages 45–49) | | |
| Session 5—The Word (pages 61–66) | | |
| Session 7—Christ the Center (pages 75–80) | | |
| Session 9—Obedience (pages 87–91) | | |
| Session 10—Fellowship (pages 93–98) | | |
| Session 11—Witness (pages 100–104) | | |
| **BOOKLET STUDIED** | | |
| *Tyranny of the Urgent* (pages 34–38) | | |
| "Summarizing *Tyranny of the Urgent*" (page 39) | | |
| **MISCELLANEOUS** | | |
| Completed an evangelism prayer list (page 82) | | |
| Completed "The Wheel and The Hand in Your Life" (page 83) | | |
| Completed "Why Memorize Scripture" (pages 99–100) | | |
| **LEADER'S CHECK** | | |
| Five entries on *My Reading Highlights* | | |
| Graduated from *Growing Strong in God's Family* | | |

# INTRODUCTION

## FOR THOSE ALREADY FAMILIAR WITH THE 2:7 SERIES

This updated version of THE 2:7 SERIES replaces the 1999 edition, which was the most current version through 2010. About 90 percent of the content is the same, but it has been sharpened and updated.

## FOR THOSE NEW TO THE 2:7 SERIES

THE 2:7 SERIES consists of three excellent workbooks designed for your group to work through and discuss. The three books are most effective when completed in sequence. Book 2 builds on the work completed in book 1, and book 3 builds on what your group has accomplished in the first two books. You will enjoy each book's biblical and practical approach to discipleship. As many others have, those of you participating in a 2:7 group can expect to experience positive life changes as you study and apply this time-proven material. Here is the main content of the three courses.

### BOOK 1: *GROWING STRONG IN GOD'S FAMILY*
Learn ways to spend personal time with God in the Bible and in prayer. Discuss helpful Bible studies and memorize key verses on principles for Christian living.

### BOOK 2: *DEEPENING YOUR ROOTS IN GOD'S FAMILY*
Memorize several classic Bible verses that you will use for a lifetime. Experience an extended time alone with God. Think through your own spiritual history so that you can express it to someone not yet committed to Christ.

### BOOK 3: *BEARING FRUIT IN GOD'S FAMILY*
Discuss Bible studies related to Christian character. Memorize verses you can use to explain the gospel to others.

## WHERE TO USE THE 2:7 SERIES

Use it with adults; use it with youth or collegiates; use it with women; use it with men. You will find it effective for one-to-one ministry, small groups, and mentoring.

THE 2:7 SERIES deals with foundational discipleship issues. You can see God use it in many contexts. It deals with the basics of the Christian life. The basics are basic, but they are also essential—for every Christian for an entire lifetime. The dynamics in THE 2:7 SERIES help people establish or stabilize the Christian basics in their everyday lives.

## GROUP LEADERS

You want one person to act as leader during each group meeting. This may be the same person each time, or the responsibility may be shared by two or three group members.

Leader's guides are available at the website www.2-7series.org for the three books in THE 2:7 SERIES. Suggestions in the leader's guides are specific and practical. It is very important to use the leader's guides as you facilitate one of these groups.

## NAVIGATOR RESOURCES AVAILABLE TO YOU

On THE 2:7 SERIES website there are helps for group participants, group leaders, and church leaders who manage discipleship training. Learn approaches that others are using to make THE 2:7 SERIES discipleship training effective.

Two ministries within The Navigators also provide practical resources and help for developing disciples and disciplemakers in your church:

- **NavPress** (www.navpress.com)—The NavPress mission is to advance The Navigators' calling by publishing life-transforming materials that are biblically rooted, culturally relevant, and highly practical.
- **Church Discipleship Ministry (CDM)** (www.navigators.org/cdm)—CDM partners with church leaders to develop generations of disciples in everyday life where they live, work, and play.

Both ministries continue to develop materials, tools, and training you can use in your personal or local church ministry. The mailing address is The Navigators, P.O. Box 6000, Colorado Springs, CO, 80934.

## ABBREVIATIONS FOR BIBLE VERSIONS

Unless otherwise identified, Scripture quotations are from the *Holy Bible*: New International Version. You can refer back to this list when you encounter unfamiliar Bible version abbreviations.

- (AMP) The Amplified Bible
- (ESV) English Standard Version
- (KJV) King James Version
- (MLB) Modern Language Bible: The Berkeley Version in Modern English
- (MSG) The Message
- (NASB) New American Standard Bible
- (NCV) New Century Version
- (NIV) New International Version
- (NKJV) New King James Version
- (NLT) New Living Translation
- (NRSV) New Revised Standard Version
- (PH) The New Testament in Modern English (J. B. Phillips)

# SESSION 1

**OUTLINE OF THIS SESSION**

1. Open the session in prayer.
2. Get acquainted with other members in your group.
3. Read "Based on Colossians 2:7" (pages 13–14) and "General Comments" (pages 14–15).
4. Learn how to make your Bible reading exciting (pages 15–18).
    a. "Why Read and Mark a Bible" (page 15)
    b. "Ways to Mark Your Bible as You Read" (pages 15–17)
    c. "Choosing Where to Read in Your Bible" (page 17)
    d. "What to Mark" (page 18)
5. Complete the "Reading and Marking Exercise" (pages 18–19).
6. Discuss "Scripture Memory Overview" (pages 19–20).
7. Glance through "*Beginning with Christ* Explanation" (pages 20–24) in preparation for its corresponding Bible study in session 2.
8. Read "Proven Ways to Memorize a Verse Effectively" (pages 24–25).
9. Read "Assignment for Session 2" (page 25).
10. Close the session in prayer.

## BASED ON COLOSSIANS 2:7

> Rooted and built up in him, strengthened in the faith as you were taught, and overflowing with thankfulness.
> —COLOSSIANS 2:7

What is the purpose of THE 2:7 SERIES? What the Holy Spirit expresses through Paul in Colossians 2:7 clearly describes the specific goals of this training:

1. **For a Christian to become** *built up* **in Christ and** *strengthened* **in his or her faith.** This series of courses includes instruction in practical Bible study, Scripture memory skills, how to sharpen one's devotional

life, and how to be more effective in evangelism. The objective is to become consistent in these disciplines rather than to just accumulate Bible knowledge.

2. **For a Christian to learn to** *overflow with thankfulness* **in everyday life**. The series will help an individual learn to experience and enjoy a stable and consistent daily walk with Christ.

3. **For a Christian to be** *taught*. The learning that strengthens our life does not come from lectures. Over time we see life transformation if we stay consistent in Scripture, listening to the promptings of the Holy Spirit and applying what we learn. The discussions can impact every member of a group in positive ways.

What are some results of THE 2:7 SERIES? Many who have worked through this series have developed qualities enabling them to assume greater responsibilities and become more effective in their local churches. Marriages and families have been helped as individual members have grown spiritually and become firmly established in their daily walk with God. After graduating from this series of courses, these maturing Christians have acquired additional tools for helping others with their growth in Christ and in reaching out to those not yet committed to Christ.

Each of the three courses consists of eleven interactive sessions. The class sessions last one to two hours. You will find THE 2:7 SERIES to be an enriching relational experience, both with those in your group and with God Himself.

## GENERAL COMMENTS

1. Ideally there should be four to twelve people in a discipleship group (including the leader). A group of this size allows time for each person in the group to participate.

2. Individuals should not join the group after session 2, because catching up would require hurrying through the material.

3. Certain requirements need to be completed to graduate from this course. While not difficult, to benefit most from each course will require purposeful effort. Plan to finish strong.

4. Keep in mind that almost anything truly worthwhile may be costly in some way.

5. Most class sessions will require about one hour of preparation time.

6. Investing time in your lesson early helps you avoid the last-minute rush. When your homework is done well, you will find that you gain the most

permanent benefit from the training.

7. It is best if you do not miss more than two sessions during this course. It becomes difficult to catch up once you get behind.

8. This is not a lecture course. You will have an opportunity to participate in every session.

## WHY READ AND MARK A BIBLE

One of the most valuable spiritual disciplines in the life of a healthy Christian is the regular reading of Scripture. Previous 2:7 groups have shown that people get more out of Bible reading when they mark ideas that catch their eye or touch their heart. You and those in your group will often experience great mutual encouragement or challenge when you share what you have read and marked.

You will find it helpful to choose an inexpensive contemporary translation or paraphrase for your reading and marking. Your group leader might suggest some options. You can also check www.2-7series.org.

## WAYS TO MARK YOUR BIBLE AS YOU READ

One option is to use a highlighter to mark words, phrases, or sentences. Most Bible bookstores sell dry highlighters or colored pencils that work well for Bible marking. (Regular highlighters can bleed through the thinner paper often found in Bibles.)

Some people like to mark with a ballpoint pen. Following are some commonly used pen markings that you might want to choose from if using a ballpoint pen.

1. **Brackets—[ ]**
   Brackets can be put around a phrase or even a sentence or two.
2. **Short diagonal lead-in—\\**
   The short diagonal lead-in refers to the phrase that immediately follows it.
3. **Parallel diagonal lines in the margin—⫽**
   Parallel diagonal lines can be used when the passage being marked is longer than one verse.
4. **Circle—◯**
   A circle can be used for repeated words within a passage or to indicate the people who are the principal characters in that passage.
5. **Vertical line in the margin—|**

A vertical line in the margin refers to the phrase or sentence(s) beside it.

6. **Underlining**—  ——

Underlining can be used for words, phrases, or a sentence. For a block of verses, other markings are less tedious than underlining.

The important point is to mark the parts of a passage that impress you either in your mind or in your heart.

The following four segments of Scripture show examples of how others have marked these passages as they were reading.

**ISAIAH 11:1-7**

A shoot will come up from the stump of Jesse; from his roots a Branch will bear fruit. ²The Spirit of the LORD will rest on him—the Spirit of wisdom and of understanding, the Spirit of counsel and of power, the Spirit of knowledge and of the fear of the LORD—³and he will delight in the fear of the LORD. He will not judge by what he sees with his eyes, or decide by what he hears with his ears; ⁴but with righteousness he will judge the needy, with justice he will give decisions for the poor of the earth. He will strike the earth with the rod of his mouth; with the breath of his lips he will slay the wicked. Righteousness will be his belt and faithfulness the sash around his waist. ⁶The wolf will live with the lamb, the leopard will lie down with the goat, the calf and the lion and the yearling together; and a little child will lead them. ⁷The cow will feed with the bear, their young will lie down together, and the lion will eat straw like the ox.

**LUKE 5:15-17**

¹⁵Yet the news about him spread all the more, so that crowds of people came to hear him and to be healed of their sicknesses. ¹⁶But Jesus often withdrew to lonely places and prayed.

¹⁷One day as he was teaching, Pharisees and teachers of the law, who had come from every village of Galilee and from Judea and Jerusalem, were sitting there. And the power of the Lord was present for him to heal the sick.

**1 KINGS 12:3-9** (MLB)

³When Jeroboam and the whole assembly of Israel arrived, they addressed Rehoboam, saying, ⁴"Your father made our yoke unbearable. Now lighten the unbearable service of your father and the heavy yoke he laid upon us, and we will serve you." ⁵He responded, "Give me three more days; then return to me."

When the people left, ⁶Rehoboam conferred with the elders who had stood by Solomon when he was still alive, saying, "How would you advise me to reply to the people? ⁷They advised him, ["If you will be a servant to this people now and serve them and reply to them with kind words, they will always be your servants."] [8]But he rejected the advice which the elders gave him. Then he conferred with the young men who grew up with him and stood by him. [9]"What do you advise us to say to this people who petitioned me, 'Make lighter the yoke your father laid upon us'?"

## 1 THESSALONIANS 1:1-7 (AMP)

[1]Paul, Silvanus (Silas), and Timothy, to the assembly (church) of the Thessalonians in God the Father and the Lord Jesus Christ (the Messiah): [Grace (spiritual blessing and divine favor) to you and [heart] peace.]

[2]We are ever giving thanks to God for all of you, continually mentioning [you when engaged] in our prayers, [3]recalling unceasingly before our God and Father your work energized by faith and service motivated by love, and unwavering hope in [the return of] our Lord Jesus Christ (the Messiah). [4][O] brethren beloved by God, we recognize *and* know that He has selected (chosen) you; [5]for our [preaching of the] glad tidings (the Gospel) came to you not only in word, but also [in [its own inherent] power] and in the Holy Spirit, and with great conviction *and* absolute certainty [on our part]. You know what kind of men we proved [ourselves] to be among you for your good. [6]And you [set yourselves to] become imitators of us and [through us] of the Lord Himself, for you welcomed our message in [spite of] much persecution, with joy [inspired] by the Holy Spirit; [7]so that you [thus] became a pattern to all the believers (those who adhere to, trust in, and rely on Christ Jesus) in Macedonia and Achaia [most of Greece].

## CHOOSING WHERE TO READ IN YOUR BIBLE

1. If reading the Bible is fairly new to you, you may find it helpful to start with a New Testament book such as John or Philippians.
2. It is better to finish reading all of one book before starting another.
3. For many, the two most difficult books in the Bible are Leviticus and Revelation. It is wise to put off reading these two books until after completing book 1 of this series.
4. Instead of reading the gospels consecutively, add variety by interspersing them with other books.
5. When you are ready to begin reading in the Old Testament, it might be helpful to start with one of the following books: Joshua, 1 Samuel, 2 Samuel, 1 Kings, 2 Kings, Genesis, or Daniel.

# WHAT TO MARK

You are not looking for the main theological teaching when you read—that would be something that's done through Bible study. Mark things you like: words of encouragement, insights, challenges, observations, or something interesting. Read for enjoyment. When you finish a chapter, go back to review what you have marked. You may see a pattern indicating something God may be bringing to your attention.

# READING AND MARKING EXERCISE

For this reading and marking exercise, you are working through Romans 12. As you do this exercise:

1. Pray that God will speak to you from His Word.
2. Think through the passage.
3. Mark the thoughts that stand out or impress you.

After you have read this passage, you will have an opportunity to share with the group one or two things that you marked.

**ROMANS 12**

[1]Therefore, I urge you, brothers, in view of God's mercy, to offer your bodies as living sacrifices, holy and pleasing to God—that is your spiritual act of worship. [2]Do not conform any longer to the pattern of this world, but be transformed by the renewing of your mind. Then you will be able to test and approve what God's will is—his good, pleasing and perfect will.

[3]For by the grace given me I say to every one of you: Do not think of yourself more highly than you ought, but rather think of yourself with sober judgment, in accordance with the measure of faith God has given you. [4]Just as each of us has one body with many members, and these members do not all have the same function, [5]so in Christ we who are many form one body, and each member belongs to all the others. [6]We have different gifts, according to the grace given us. If a man's gift is prophesying, let him use it in proportion to his faith. [7]If it is serving, let him serve; if it is teaching, let him teach, [8]if it is encouraging, let him encourage; if it is contributing to the needs of others, let him give generously; if it is leadership, let him govern diligently; if it is showing mercy, let him do it cheerfully.

[9]Love must be sincere. Hate what is evil; cling to what is good. [10]Be devoted to one another in brotherly

love. Honor one another above yourselves. [11]Never be lacking in zeal, but keep your spiritual fervor, serving the Lord. [12]Be joyful in hope, patient in affliction, faithful in prayer. [13]Share with God's people who are in need. Practice hospitality.

[14]Bless those who persecute you; bless and do not curse. [15]Rejoice with those who rejoice; mourn with those who mourn. [16]Live in harmony with one another. Do not be proud, but be willing to associate with people of low position. Do not be conceited. - proud arrogant

[17]Do not repay anyone evil for evil. Be careful to do what is right in the eyes of everybody. [18]If it is possible, as far as it depends on you, live at peace with everyone. [19]Do not take revenge, my friends, but leave room for God's wrath, for it is written: "It is mine to avenge; I will repay," says the Lord. [20]On the contrary: "If your enemy is hungry, feed him; if he is thirsty, give him something to drink. In doing this, you will heap burning coals on his head." [21]Do not be overcome by evil, but overcome evil with good.

## SCRIPTURE MEMORY OVERVIEW

During this course, you will memorize five important passages of Scripture. For years to come, you will find key memorized verses to be helpful in your own life and for helping others. As you memorize each passage, you will also memorize the topic and the Bible reference. The verses are taken from The Navigator's Scripture memory packet called *Beginning with Christ*. Here are the topics and references.

| | |
|---|---|
| Assurance of Salvation | 1 John 5:11-12 |
| Assurance of Answered Prayer | John 16:24 |
| Assurance of Victory | 1 Corinthians 10:13 |
| Assurance of Forgiveness | 1 John 1:9 |
| Assurance of Guidance | Proverbs 3:5-6 |

Consider also memorizing John 5:24. It is a very helpful verse for you to use when you are explaining your faith to someone. It can actually become a one-verse gospel explanation.

### CHOOSING A TRANSLATION FOR SCRIPTURE MEMORY
Sometimes a paraphrase or expanded version of the Bible presents a particular verse or passage in a dynamic way. Many people have memorized 1 Corinthians 13:4-8 in the Phillips paraphrase for that reason. Numbers of women have been

blessed by memorizing Proverbs 31 in the Amplified Bible. The usual guideline is to do your memory work using a translation of the Bible rather than a paraphrase.

Your group will discuss translations from which you can choose to do your memory work (see pages 109–113 in the appendix). Often people choose the translation used by their pastor or the one most used in their church. Think about it. Talk to others and decide.

### CHOOSING SCRIPTURE MEMORY CARDS

At www.2-7series.org, you can download the memory verses for this course and print them on cards, or you may choose to write your verses on blank cards. Blank business cards are available at office supply stores and at print shops. Some Christian bookstores carry them. Another option that some people prefer is to use 3x5 index cards.

If you choose to use blank cards, on the front of the card, write the topic, the reference, the verse, and the reference at the bottom. You will find that having the memory verses on cards makes memorizing and reviewing easier.

We suggest that you write the topic and reference on the back of the card. In this way, you can review your learned verses by first looking at the topic and reference on the back of the card and then flipping the card over to check your accuracy.

Start out by using the guidelines this course suggests for memorizing and reviewing. By the end of this training, you will have established a pattern that works well for you.

By carrying your verses in a verse pack, you can use spare moments to memorize and review. At www.2-7series.org you can find information about verse cards, verse packs, and other Scripture memory tools.

For the next class, you will be memorizing "Assurance of Salvation," 1 John 5:11-12. The following section, *"Beginning with Christ* Explanation," describes the purpose for memorizing these five BWC passages: first for your own assurance, and then for giving assurance to others.

## *BEGINNING WITH CHRIST* EXPLANATION

The Bible says that "if you confess with your mouth, 'Jesus is Lord,' and believe in your heart that God raised him from the dead, you will be saved. For it is with your heart that you believe and are justified, and it is with your mouth that you confess and are saved" (**Romans 10:9-10**). Coupled with this wonderful truth is the statement in His Word that "to all who received him, to those who believed in his name, he gave the right to become children of God" (**John 1:12**).

According to these Scriptures, if you have to the best of your knowledge received Jesus Christ (trusted Him as your own Savior), you have become a child of God in whom Jesus Christ dwells.

Many people make the mistake of measuring the certainty of their salvation by their feelings. Don't make this tragic mistake. Believe God. Take Him at His Word: "I write these things to you who believe in the name of the Son of God so that you may know that you have eternal life" (**1 John 5:13**).

It is impossible in these few pages to go into all the wonderful results of the transaction that took place when you received Christ. Children may be born into a wealthy home and become the possessor of good parents, brothers and sisters, houses and lands, but at the time of their birth it is not necessary that they be informed of all these wonderful things. There are more important matters to take care of first. They must be protected, for they have been born into a world with many enemies. In the hospital room, they are handled with sterilized gloves and kept from outsiders to prevent them from falling victim to the myriad germs and viruses waiting to attack. It is the awareness of such enemies that enables the doctors and nurses to take measures to protect the precious new life.

You have become a child of God; you have been born into His family as a spiritual babe. This is a strategic moment in your life. The following basic truths will strengthen you for the battle ahead and keep you safe from the onslaughts of Satan.

In 1 Peter 2:2 we read, "Like newborn babies, crave pure spiritual milk, so that by it you may grow up in your salvation." In **Acts 20:32** we read, "Now I commit you to God and to the word of his grace, which can build you up." The Bible serves as our spiritual food and will build us up in the faith. In this course, you are given suggestions for how to read your Bible. It is important that you have time set aside, preferably in the morning, to read the Word of God and pray.

Now let's be more specific with regard to your intake of the Word of God. In **Psalm 119**, it says, "How can a young man keep his way pure?" (verse 9), and then the psalmist speaks to the Lord, saying, "I have hidden your word in my heart that I might not sin against you" (**verse 11**). So we hide His Word in our heart by memorizing key passages. This course offers five useful Scripture passages with which you may begin.

Let us consider for a moment the spiritual Enemy you face. Before you trusted Christ, Satan may not have bothered you particularly, but now he has seen you make the step that angers him more than any one thing in all the world: You have left his crowd and joined the ranks of those who believe and trust in the Son of God. You are no longer in Satan's domain; you now belong to the One who has bought and paid for you with a price, the price of His own blood, shed on the cross. You may be sure that Satan will attempt to trouble you. His attacks assume many forms. These memory verses will help you deal with some of the most common satanic attacks and give you help on how to resist him successfully.

You can overcome him only as you use the weapons God has provided. Paul said, "Take . . . the sword of the Spirit, which is the word of God" (**Ephesians 6:17**). The Bible, then, is the primary weapon against these attacks.

Consider that Jesus Christ was tempted by Satan in three specific ways, and He defeated him each time with Scripture, saying, "It is written" (see Matthew 4). If Christ deemed it necessary to meet Satan this way, how much more do we need this mighty weapon, the Word of God? How much more do we need to be prepared to say to Satan, "It is written" or "Thus said the Lord"?

### 1. Assurance of Salvation

The memory verses of Scripture in this course have been chosen to give you a defense against some of the most common attacks from the Enemy. Often Satan's first approach is to cast doubt upon the work God has done in your heart. You may find yourself thinking, *How can I be saved and my sins forgiven just by believing and receiving Christ? Surely that is not enough!*

Your only hope to withstand such an attack is to resort to God's Word. What does God say about the matter? That is the important thing. And so the first memory passage, **1 John 5:11-12** (Assurance of Salvation), says, "And this is the testimony: God has given us eternal life, and this life is in his Son. He who has the Son has life; he who does not have the Son of God does not have life."

When this passage has been written on the table of your heart, you will be able to use it every time a doubt arises. On the basis of God's written Word, you will have overcome one of the first tests. This attack may recur, but now you can use the Word of God in your heart to meet it.

### 2. Assurance of Answered Prayer

Another attack of Satan may be to cause you to doubt the effectiveness of prayer. You may catch yourself thinking, *How can God really be personally interested in me? He seems far away and is probably concerned about more important things. When I pray, does He hear me, much less answer my prayers?*

With Jesus Christ as your Savior and Lord, you have the unique privilege of speaking directly with your heavenly Father through Him. God wants you to come confidently into His presence. "Let us then approach the throne of grace with confidence"

(Hebrews 4:16) and to talk to Him about everything. "Do not be anxious about anything, but in everything, by prayer and petition, with thanksgiving, present your requests to God" (Philippians 4:6). He is intensely interested in you and your needs.

In the second passage, John 16:24, Jesus gives us His assurance of answered prayer: "Until now you have not asked for anything in my name. Ask and you will receive, and your joy will be complete."

Jesus did not say that His disciples had never asked before. You yourself have probably asked many times, especially when in trouble. But now you can ask in Jesus' name because you belong to Him. To ask in His name means to ask in His authority and on His merit. Just as the Father answered Jesus' every prayer, so will He answer your call and meet your needs. Memorize this wonderful promise. Apply its truth and experience the joy of answered prayer.

### 3. Assurance of Victory

Still another attack may be along this line: *I have spiritual life, all right, but in my following God, I feel that I am a weakling; I have always been weak.*

You will remember some sin that has gripped you throughout the past years of your life. You will think, *I am weak; I will not be able to stand against this particular temptation. Perhaps I am able to stand against others, but not this one.*

How will you answer this doubt? Will you rely on what this person or that one says, or will you resort to the invincible Word? The third passage, **1 Corinthians 10:13**, is chosen especially to meet this attack of Satan: "No temptation has seized you except what is common to man. And God is faithful; he will not let you be tempted beyond what you can bear. But when you are tempted, he will also provide a way out so that you can stand up under it."

This verse gives assurance of victory. Our faithful God promises victory over temptation. It belongs to you as a child of His. He will always give you an "exit" to avoid sin. Believe what God has said and you will see that things impossible with men are possible with God. It will thrill you to see that chains of lifetime habits can be broken by His mighty power. Memorize this verse; write it on the table of your heart and then trust the Holy Spirit to help you live victoriously over sin.

### 4. Assurance of Forgiveness

This brings us to the next attack of Satan. Although victory over temptation is rightfully yours, you may fail. When you sin, you may think, *Now I've done it. I'm supposed to be a Christian, but Christians don't do those things, do they?*

Nevertheless, God makes provision in His Word for the failures of His children, and so the fourth passage, **1 John 1:9**, speaks of the assurance of forgiveness: "If we confess our sins, he is faithful and just and will forgive us our sins and purify us from all unrighteousness."

To confess a sin means to uncover it by calling it exactly what God calls it: sin. You "tell it like it is" to God. Implicit in honest confession is the willingness to forsake the sin. "He who conceals his sins does not prosper, but whoever confesses and renounces them finds mercy" (Proverbs 28:13). God promises to not only forgive us but also cleanse us. What a gracious provision! You can thank God for His forgiveness. When we are honest and repent, God gives us a fresh start!

### 5. Assurance of Guidance
The four preceding assurances have been given to help you meet the principal attacks of Satan. However, the fifth passage for you to memorize is for a different purpose.

You may have questions about the future, wondering how this new life of yours is all going to work out. *What about God's will for my life? Will He really lead me?* This verse (**Proverbs 3:5-6**) comes to give you assurance of guidance: "Trust in the LORD with all your heart and lean not on your own understanding; in all your ways acknowledge him, and he will make your paths straight."

God promises to lead you and direct your path when you rely on Him completely. Memorize and apply this Scripture as a reminder to trust God for His guidance in your life.

After you have memorized these verses and learned to apply them, you will be aware of the strength and blessings that come from hiding God's Word in your heart.

## PROVEN WAYS TO MEMORIZE A VERSE EFFECTIVELY

1. Before you start to memorize the verse, read it aloud several times.
2. Learn the topic, reference, and first phrase as a unit.
3. After you have reviewed the topic, reference, and first phrase a few times, add the second phrase. Gradually add phrases until you know the whole verse. (It is best to do this over a period of several hours.)
4. Work on the verses audibly whenever possible.
5. As you memorize and review the verse, think about how it applies to your own life.
6. Always review the verse in this sequence:
   a. TOPIC: "Assurance of Salvation"
   b. REFERENCE: "First John five, eleven and twelve"
   c. VERSE(S): "And this is the testimony: God has given us eternal life, and this life is in his Son. He who has the Son has life; he who does not

have the Son of God does not have life."

    d. REFERENCE: "First John five, eleven and twelve"

7. The most critical element in Scripture memory is review, review, review! The most important time to review a verse repeatedly is right after you can quote the whole verse (topic, reference, verse, reference) without making a mistake. Review the verse preferably many times a day for several days. After that, plan to review the verses once a day during this course. The more you review, the greater your retention.

8. An important concept is the principle of over-learning. We can recall names, phone numbers, web addresses, and routes to certain stores or homes because we have "over-learned" them—the information is deeply planted in our memory. So in doing Scripture memory, we don't consider a verse memorized simply at the point when we can quote it accurately. Only after having reviewed it frequently enough for it to become ingrained in our memory can we say with certainty that a verse has been memorized.

## ASSIGNMENT FOR SESSION 2

1. Scripture Memory: Carefully read "*Beginning with Christ* Explanation" (pages 20–24). Memorize the passage on "Assurance of Salvation," 1 John 5:11-12.

2. Bible Reading: Obtain a contemporary translation or paraphrase of the Bible. Plan to read and mark in it each day. Much of session 2 is given to having group members share things they have read and marked.

3. Bible Study: Complete "*Beginning with Christ Bible Study*" (pages 28–32).

# SESSION 2

**OUTLINE OF THIS SESSION**

1. Open the session in prayer.
2. Get further acquainted with one another.
3. Review session 1.
4. Share with the rest of your group what you have read and marked in your Bible this week.
5. Break into small groups of two or three to review your memory verse, 1 John 5:11-12.
6. Review memory methods (pages 24–25):
   a. Practice aloud.
   b. Spot and correct repeated errors.
   c. Review is the key. Plan to do it daily!
7. Discuss the value of The Bridge Illustration (see pages 115–121 in the appendix).
8. Read "Introduction to Bible Study" (pages 27–28) and glance over the session 3 Bible study, "Prayer: Part 1" (pages 40–42).
9. Discuss "*Beginning with Christ Bible Study*" (pages 28–32).
10. Read "Assignment for Session 3" (page 32).
11. Close the session in prayer.

## INTRODUCTION TO BIBLE STUDY

About 925 million people in the world go to bed hungry.[1] Many Christian missions work to help solve this terrible crisis in the name of Christ. Perhaps equally tragic is the number of people who go through life spiritually undernourished. The words Christ spoke centuries ago are still true: "People do not live by bread alone, but by every word that comes from the mouth of God" (Matthew 4:4, NLT).

Because they recognize this hunger of heart that only God's Word can satisfy, more and more people are turning to serious study of the Bible. Both those new to the Christian faith and those who have known Christ for many years need this divinely appointed food for spiritual health and growth.

*Growing Strong in God's Family* Bible studies have been carefully designed to help you:

- Establish a program of personal study of God's Word
- Examine the great truths of the Bible
- Learn and practice the essentials of discipleship

To begin, all you need is a Bible. The questions in book 1 will direct you to a passage of Scripture. After considering the Scripture, write an answer in your own words. As you may know, Scripture references give the book, chapter, and verse(s). For example, Acts 20:32 refers to the book of Acts, chapter 20, verse 32.

Start your study by praying, asking for insights and for understanding: "Open my eyes that I may see wonderful things in your law" (Psalm 119:18).

For your personal Bible study, you need:

**A TIME:** Just as church attendance is planned for a regular time each week, it is helpful to plan a time for your Bible study and lesson preparation. Some like to study a little every day; others set aside an evening each week. Decide on a time that is best for you.

**A PLACE:** Choose a place free from things that distract you. If possible, study in the same place each time.

**METHOD:** As you consider each verse of Scripture, give it some careful thought, then write out an answer in your own words. (Reading the context—the surrounding verses—may give you further insight into the verse).

**MATERIAL:** Besides your 2:7 book, you need a complete Bible—Old and New Testaments. For Bible study a translation is preferred, but for your reading and marking a paraphrase works fine.

## *BEGINNING WITH CHRIST BIBLE STUDY*

Complete the following questions based on your reading of "*Beginning with Christ* Explanation" (pages 20–24). You will find answers on the pages indicated.

1. The five topics and references of the memory verses in *Growing Strong in God's Family* are:

|  | TOPIC | REFERENCE |
|---|---|---|
| Assurance of | _____ | _____ |
| Assurance of | _____ | _____ |
| Assurance of | _____ | _____ |
| Assurance of | _____ | _____ |
| Assurance of | _____ | _____ |

2. Please complete this sentence (page 21): (1 John 5:13) "Many people make the mistake of measuring the certainty of their salvation _____ _____."

3. What are one or two key ideas that you see in Romans 10:9-10 (see this verse on page 20)?

_____

_____

4. What is one of the key ideas you see in John 1:12 (pages 20–21)?

_____

_____

5. Please complete this sentence (page 21): (Acts 20:32) "The Bible serves as our _____ and will _____

_____ in the faith."

6. The psalmist said, "I have hidden your word in my heart" (Psalm 119:11). What do you think that means (page 21)?

_____

_____

7. What effective weapon has God provided for use against Satan's attacks (see Ephesians 6:17, page 22)?

_____

_____

8. What did Jesus say to Satan in a time of temptation (page 22)?

_____

_____

The five verses you memorize and study in *Growing Strong in God's Family* will help equip you for your encounters with our enemy, Satan. The following questions give you more insight into the five topics of those verses.

## ASSURANCE OF SALVATION

9. Read John 17:3. How did Jesus define eternal life?

   _____

   _____

10. Explore 1 John 5:11-12 on page 22. (The following answers are simple but profound.)

    a. Who gives eternal life? _____

    b. Where is eternal life found? _____

    c. Who has eternal life? _____

    d. Who does not have eternal life? _____

    What are one or two thoughts or feelings that you have as you glance back over your four answers?

    _____

    _____

## ASSURANCE OF ANSWERED PRAYER

11. In your own words, how would you describe prayer?

    _____

    _____

12. Explore John 16:24 (page 23).

    a. What did Jesus identify as a major need in the disciples' lives?

    _____

    _____

    b. In whose name should we pray and why?

    _____

    _____

    c. What results from prayer?

    _____

    _____

## ASSURANCE OF VICTORY

13. How would you define temptation?

14. Explore 1 Corinthians 10:13 (page 23). This verse points the way to more consistent victory over temptations and sins.
    a. According to the verse, what is true about every temptation we face?

    b. According to the verse, in what ways does God help us when we are tempted?

## ASSURANCE OF FORGIVENESS

15. Why do you think forgiveness is important?

16. Explore 1 John 1:9 (pages 23–24).
    a. What does God want you to do if you sin?

    b. What does it mean to confess?

    c. In His act of forgiving us, how is God described?

    d. What else does God do when you confess sin?

**ASSURANCE OF GUIDANCE**

17. What are some ways you have seen God guide people?

_____

_____

_____

_____

18. Explore Proverbs 3:5-6 (page 24).

    a. What three things are we told to do?

    1) _____

    2) _____

    3) _____

    b. When these conditions are met, what are you promised?

    _____

    _____

**ASSIGNMENT FOR SESSION 3**

1. Scripture Memory: Memorize the verse on "Assurance of Answered Prayer," John 16:24.
2. Bible Reading: Continue reading and marking your Bible.
3. Bible Study: Complete the Bible study "Prayer: Part 1" (pages 40–42).
4. Other: Carefully read and mark the article *Tyranny of the Urgent*, by Charles E. Hummel (pages 34–38). Please complete numbers 1, 2, and 3 for "Summarizing *Tyranny of the Urgent*" (page 39).

# SESSION 3

**OUTLINE OF THIS SESSION**

1. Open the session in prayer.
2. Study "An Effective Way to Review Memory Verses Together" (pages 33–34).
3. Break into groups of two or three and review your memory verses.
   a. "Assurance of Salvation" (1 John 5:11-12)
   b. "Assurance of Answered Prayer" (John 16:24)
4. Share with the rest of the group something you have read and marked in your Bible this week.
5. Discuss the article *Tyranny of the Urgent* (pages 34–38).
6. Discuss "Summarizing *Tyranny of the Urgent*" (page 39).
7. Discuss the Bible study "Prayer: Part 1" (pages 40–42).
8. Go over "How to Use *My Reading Progress*" (pages 42–43).
9. Read "Assignment for Session 4" (page 43).
10. Close the session in prayer.

## AN EFFECTIVE WAY TO REVIEW MEMORY VERSES TOGETHER

1. You may find it helpful to quote the memory verses you know best first. This helps to build confidence.
2. Maintain an attitude of helpfulness, encouragement, and praise. Do all you can to encourage each other's success.

> Two are better than one because they have a good return for their labor. For if either of them falls, the one will lift up his companion. But woe to the one who falls when there is not another to lift him up.
>
> —ECCLESIASTES 4:9-10 (NASB)

3. Your minimum goal is to know each verse word perfectly because:
   a. Often your ability to quote a verse perfectly will give others confidence in you so that you can help them.

b. It is mentally easier to retain a verse that has been learned perfectly.

c. If you know the content vaguely or don't know the location of the verse, what you say will have less authority.

d. Anything worth doing is worth doing well.

> Whatever your task is, put your whole heart and soul into it,
> as into work done for the Lord and not merely for men.
> —COLOSSIANS 3:23 (PH)

4. When listening, signal the quoter when he or she makes a mistake, but give verbal help only when asked.

5. After a quoter has corrected a mistake, have him or her repeat the verse word perfect before going on to another verse.

6. It works best to review your verses with someone using the same translation.

## TYRANNY OF THE URGENT

### Charles E. Hummel

Have you ever wished for a thirty-hour day? Surely this extra time would relieve the tremendous pressure under which we live. Our lives leave a trail of unfinished tasks. Unanswered letters, unvisited friends, unread books haunt quiet moments when we stop to evaluate what we have accomplished. We desperately need relief.

But would that longer day really solve our problem? Wouldn't we soon be just as frustrated as we are now with our twenty-four-hour allotment? We could hardly escape Parkinson's Principle: Work expands to fill all the available time.

Nor will the passage of time necessarily help us catch up. Children grow in number and age to require more of our time. Greater experience in profession and church brings more exacting assignments. We find ourselves working more and enjoying it less.

**JUMBLED PRIORITIES?**

When we stop long enough to think about it, we realize that our dilemma goes deeper than shortage of time; it is basically a problem of priorities. Hard work doesn't hurt us. We all know what it is to go full speed for long hours, totally involved in an important task. The resulting weariness is matched by a sense of achievement and joy. Not hard work, but doubt and misgiving produce anxiety as we review a month or a year and become oppressed by the pile of unfinished tasks. We sense uneasily our failure to do what was really important. The winds of other people's demands, and our own inner compulsions, have driven us onto a reef of frustration. We confess, quite apart from our sins, "We have done those things which we ought not to have done, and we have left undone those things which we ought to have done."

An experienced factory manager once said to me, "Your greatest danger is letting the urgent things crowd out the important." He didn't realize how hard his advice hit. It has often returned to haunt and rebuke me by raising the critical problem of priorities.

We live in constant tension between the urgent and the important. The problem is that many important tasks need not be done today, or even this week. Extra hours of prayer and Bible study, a visit to an elderly friend, reading an important book: these activities can usually wait a while longer. But often urgent, though less important, tasks call for immediate response—endless demands pressure every waking hour.

A person's home is no longer a castle, a private place away from urgent tasks. The telephone breaches its walls with incessant demands. The appeal of these demands seems irresistible, and they devour our energy. But in the light of eternity their momentary prominence fades. With a sense of loss we recall the important tasks that have been shunted aside. We realize that we've become slaves to the tyranny of the urgent. Is there any escape from this pattern of living? The answer lies in the life of our Lord.

## THE EXAMPLE OF JESUS

On the night before he died, Jesus made an astonishing claim. In his great prayer of John 17 he said to his Father, "I have brought you glory on earth by completing the work you gave me to do" (verse 4).

We wonder how Jesus could have talked about a completed work. His three-year ministry seemed all too short. A prostitute at Simon's banquet had found forgiveness and a new life, but many others still plied their trade. For every ten withered muscles that had flexed into health, a hundred remained impotent. The blind, maimed and diseased abounded throughout the land. Yet on that last night, with many urgent human needs unmet and useful tasks undone, the Lord had peace; He knew he had completed the work *God* had given him.

The Gospel records show that Jesus worked hard. After describing a busy day Mark reports, "That evening after sunset, the people brought to Jesus all the sick and demon-possessed. The whole town gathered at the door, and Jesus healed many who had various diseases. He also drove out many demons" (Mark 1:32-34).

On another occasion the demands

of the sick and maimed kept Jesus and his disciples so busy that they were not even able to eat. His family went to take charge of him, concluding that he was out of his mind (Mark 3:20-21). After yet another strenuous teaching session, Jesus and his disciples left the crowd and boarded a boat. "A furious squall came up, and the waves broke over the boat, so that it was nearly swamped." Through it all Jesus was sleeping in the stern on a cushion (Mark 4:35-38). What a picture of exhaustion!

Yet Jesus' life was never feverish; he had time for people. He could spend hours talking with one person, such as the Samaritan woman at the well (John 4). His life showed a wonderful balance, a sense of timing. On one occasion his brothers urged him to go to Judea. Jesus replied, "The right time for me has not yet come; for you any time is right" (John 7:6).

In *The Discipline and Culture of the Spiritual Life*, A. E. Whiteham observes, "Here in this Man is adequate purpose . . . inward rest, that gives an air of leisure to His crowded life. Above all there is in this Man a secret and a power of dealing with the waste-products of life, the waste of pain, disappointment, enmity, death . . . making a short life of about thirty years, abruptly cut off, to be a 'finished' life. We cannot admire the poise and beauty of this human life, and then ignore the things that made it."

## WAIT FOR INSTRUCTIONS

What was the secret of Jesus' ministry? We discover a clue in Mark's report of what happened after the very busy day of teaching and healing which we first noted. "Very early in the morning, while it was still dark, Jesus got up, left the house and went off to a solitary place, where he prayed" (Mark 1:35). *He prayerfully waited for his Father's instructions.* Jesus had no divinely drawn blueprint or schedule; he discerned the Father's will day by day in a life of prayer. Because of this he was able to resist the urgent demands of others and do what was really important for his mission.

In the middle of a fruitful ministry across the Jordan where John the Baptist had preached, Jesus received an urgent message from his close friends Mary and Martha concerning their brother Lazarus: "Lord, the one you love is sick" (John 11:3). John records the Lord's paradoxical response: "Jesus loved Martha and her sister and Lazarus. Yet when he heard that Lazarus was sick, he stayed where he was two more days" (verses 5-6).

The urgent need was to prevent the death of the beloved brother. But the important thing from God's point of view was to raise Lazarus from the dead. So he was allowed to die and his sisters to grieve. Then Jesus traveled to Bethany and also wept with the family. He raised Lazarus, having proclaimed: "I am the resurrection and the life. He who believes in me will live, even though he dies" (verse 25).

We may wonder why our Lord's ministry was so short, why it could not have lasted another five or ten years, why so many wretched sufferers were left in their misery. Since Scripture gives no answer to these questions, we must leave them within the mystery of God's purposes. But we do know that Jesus' prayerful waiting for the Father's instruction freed him from the tyranny of the urgent. It gave him a sense of direction, set a steady pace and at the end of his earthly ministry gave him the satisfaction that he had completed the work God had assigned him to do.

**DEPENDENCE MAKES YOU FREE**
Freedom from tyranny of the urgent is found not only in the example of our Lord but also in his promise. In a vigorous debate with the Pharisees in Jerusalem, Jesus said to those who believed in him: "If you hold to my teaching, you are really my disciples. Then you will know the truth, and the truth will set you free. . . . I tell you the truth, everyone who sins is a slave to sin. . . . If the Son sets you free, you will be free indeed" (John 8:31-32,34,36).

Many of us have experienced Christ's deliverance from the penalty and power of sin in our lives. Are we also letting him free us from the tyranny of the urgent? In this message he points the way: "If you hold to my teaching." This is the path to freedom, continuing day by day to meditate on the Scriptures and gain our Lord's perspective.

P. T. Forsyth once said, "The worst sin is prayerlessness." Does this statement surprise us? We usually think of murder and adultery as among the worst offenses against God and humanity. But the root of all sin is self-sufficiency—independence from the rule of God. When we fail to wait prayerfully for God's guidance and strength, we are saying with our actions, if not with our words, that we do not need him. How much of our service is actually a "going it alone"?

The opposite of such independence is prayer in which we acknowledge our need of God's guidance and empowerment. In this respect we have seen the example set by Jesus in the Gospels. He lived and served in complete dependence on his Father. Contrary to popular views, such dependence does not limit or repress human personality. We are never so fully personal—free to become our true selves—as when we are living in complete dependence on God.

**EVALUATE**
People in business recognize the need to evaulate the present and plan for the future. Former President Greenwalt of DuPont said, "One minute spent in planning saves three or four minutes in execution." Many in sales have multiplied their profits by setting aside Friday afternoon to

plan carefully the major activities of the coming week. Executives who are too busy to stop and plan may find themselves replaced by others who know better. Christians who are too busy to stop, take spiritual inventory, and receive their assignments from God become slaves to the tyranny of the urgent. They may work day and night to achieve much that seems significant to themselves and others, but they don't complete the work God has for them to do.

In addition to your daily quiet time, set aside one hour a week for spiritual inventory. Jot down an evaluation of the past, record any lessons God may be teaching you, and plan your activities for the coming week. Also try to set aside a few hours each month for a longer-range evaluation and planning. Often you may fail. Ironically, the busier we get, the more we need these periods—and the less we seem able to schedule them. We become like the fanatic who, unsure of his direction, doubles his speed.

Prayerful waiting on God is indispensable to effective service. Like the time-out in a basketball game, it enables us to catch our breath and reevaluate our strategy. In prayer we learn the truth about God, ourselves, and the tasks he wants us to undertake. The *need* itself, however urgent, is not the *call* for us to meet it; the call must come from the Lord who knows our limitations. "The LORD has compassion on those who fear him; for he knows how we are formed, he remembers that we are dust" (Psalm 103:13-14). It is not God who loads us until we bend or break with an ulcer, heart attack or stroke. These largely come from our inner compulsions under the pressure of external demands.

## CONTINUE THE EFFORT

Over the years I have found that one of the greatest struggles in the Christian life is the effort to make adequate time for daily waiting on God, weekly inventory and monthly planning. Yet this is the path to escaping the tyranny of the urgent. As we hold to the teachings of Jesus and seek his wisdom in the decisions we make, he frees us from the tyranny of the urgent to do what is really important.

Nothing substitutes for knowing that on this day, at this hour, in this place, we are doing the will of our Father in heaven. Only then can we contemplate in peace so many unfinished tasks. At the end of our lives, whether they are short or long, what could give us greater joy than being sure that we have completed the work God gave us to do? Then we can look forward to seeing our Lord and hearing him say, "Well done, good and faithful servant!" (Matthew 25:21).

# SUMMARIZING *TYRANNY OF THE URGENT*

It seems to me that perfection of means and confusion of
goals seem to characterize our age.

—ALBERT EINSTEIN

The good is often the enemy of the best.

—UNKNOWN

1. Define the word *urgent* as used in *Tyranny of the Urgent*.

   _____

   _____

2. Define the word *important* as used in *Tyranny of the Urgent*.

   _____

   _____

3. What are some of the thoughts that most impressed you in *Tyranny of*
   *the Urgent*? _____

   _____

   _____

   _____

4. As you discuss *Tyranny of the Urgent*, what are some of the best thoughts
   that others share in your group?

   _____

   _____

   _____

   _____

Assignments in this course are not long, but you want to allow sixty to ninety
minutes of preparation time for most sessions. Start early! You may find it
helpful to plan when and where you will work on your assignments.

   a. Reading and marking daily   Time _____

                                              Place _____

   b. Scripture memory daily   Time _____

                                              Place _____

c. Assignments in this book    Time _____

Place _____

On what days of the week? _____

# PRAYER: PART 1

Communication is essential for a growing relationship. When you pray, the Holy Spirit helps you know what to say and how to say it (Romans 8:26-27).

> The great people of the earth today are the people who pray. I do not mean those who talk about prayer, not those who can explain about prayer, but I mean those people who take time and pray. They have not time. It must be taken from something else. This something else is important— very important and pressing, but still less important and less pressing than prayer.
>
> —S. D. GORDON

> The Spirit links Himself with us in our praying and pours His supplication into our own. We may master the technique of prayer and understand its philosophy; we may have unlimited confidence in the veracity and validity of the promises concerning prayer. We may plead them earnestly. But if we ignore the part played by the Holy Spirit, we have failed to use the master key.
>
> —J. OSWALD SANDERS

### THINK ABOUT:

Apart from salvation what is the biggest thing for which you have ever prayed and the greatest answer you have ever received?

_____

_____

## PRAYER—YOUR COMMUNICATION TO GOD

1. As a believer, you enjoy a relationship with Christ and have been given a

special privilege. What is this privilege and why was it given (Hebrews 4:16)? _____

_____

_____

2. Because God is the believer's refuge, what are you told to do (Psalm 62:8)? _____

_____

_____

What could hinder a person from doing this? _____

_____

3. Different types of prayer help us communicate the variety of thoughts we want to pray. Fill in the chart using the following verses. First, write in the reference of the "praise" verse, and then make up a sentence prayer that is an example of praise. Please do that for each of the five types of prayer.

- Psalm 38:18: "I confess my iniquity; I am troubled by my sin."
- Hebrews 13:15: "Through Jesus, therefore, let us continually offer to God a sacrifice of praise—the fruit of lips that confess his name."
- Luke 11:3: "Give us each day our daily bread."
- Ephesians 5:20: "Always giving thanks to God the Father for everything, in the name of our Lord Jesus Christ."
- James 5:16: "Therefore confess your sins to each other and pray for each other so that you may be healed."

| TYPE | VERSE REFERENCE | MAKE UP AN EXAMPLE |
|------|-----------------|--------------------|
| Praise | 1. _____ | _____ |
| | | _____ |
| Thanksgiving | 2. _____ | _____ |
| | | _____ |
| Confession | 3. _____ | _____ |
| | | _____ |
| Intercession | 4. _____ | _____ |
| | | _____ |

Supplication    5. _____    _____

_____

**THE PRACTICE OF PRAYER**

4.  What conditions for prayer do you find in the following verses?

Psalms 66:18 _____

_____

Matthew 21:22 _____

_____

John 15:7 _____

_____

(Some translations say *abide*, meaning to continue, remain, dwell, or endure.)

John 16:24 _____

_____

1 John 5:14-15 _____

_____

James 4:3 _____

_____

Even when conditions are met, it sometimes appears as if God is not answering prayer. But remember that "No" and "Wait" are as much an answer as "Yes."

## HOW TO USE *MY READING PROGRESS*

You will find a copy of *My Reading Progress* on pages 153–154. Online you may download an additional copy whenever you need one (www.2-7series.org). *My Reading Progress* is a method for keeping track of the Bible book and chapter you are reading. You will find it both helpful and encouraging to use.

As you can see on *My Reading Progress*, the books of the Bible are listed in the order in which they appear in Scripture. The Old and New Testaments are listed separately. The numbers that follow each book title represent the number of chapters in that book. For example, the book of Romans has sixteen chapters, so you see sixteen numerals printed after the word *Romans*.

Sample segment from *My Reading Progress*:

| | | | | | | | | | | | | | | | | | | | | | |
|---|---|---|---|---|---|---|---|---|---|---|---|---|---|---|---|---|---|---|---|---|---|
| Matthew | 1 | 2 | 3 | 4 | 5 | 6 | 7 | 8 | 9 | 10 | 11 | 12 | 13 | 14 | 15 | 16 | 17 | 18 | 19 | 20 | 21 |
| | 22 | 23 | 24 | 25 | 26 | 27 | 28 | | | | | | | | | | | | | | |
| Mark | 1 | 2 | 3 | 4 | 5 | 6 | 7 | 8 | 9 | 10 | 11 | 12 | 13 | 14 | 15 | 16 | | | | | |
| Luke | 1 | 2 | 3 | 4 | 5 | 6 | 7 | 8 | 9 | 10 | 11 | 12 | 13 | 14 | 15 | 16 | 17 | 18 | 19 | 20 | 21 |
| | 22 | 23 | 24 | | | | | | | | | | | | | | | | | | |
| John | 1 | 2 | 3 | 4 | 5 | 6 | 7 | 8 | 9 | 10 | 11 | 12 | 13 | 14 | 15 | 16 | 17 | 18 | 19 | 20 | 21 |
| Acts | 1 | 2 | 3 | 4 | 5 | 6 | 7 | 8 | 9 | 10 | 11 | 12 | 13 | 14 | 15 | 16 | 17 | 18 | 19 | 20 | 21 |
| | 22 | 23 | 24 | 25 | 26 | 27 | 28 | | | | | | | | | | | | | | |
| **Romans** | **1** | **2** | **3** | **4** | **5** | **6** | **7** | **8** | **9** | **10** | **11** | **12** | **13** | **14** | **15** | **16** | | | | | |

If today you read the first two chapters of Romans, you draw a diagonal line or an "X" through numerals 1 and 2. You can continue marking this way until you complete the book. Some people prefer to mark off all the chapters when they finish reading a book.

**Romans** ~~1~~ ~~2~~ **3 4 5 6 7 8 9 10 11 12 13 14 15 16**

**or**

**Romans** X X **3 4 5 6 7 8 9 10 11 12 13 14 15 16**

When you finish reading a book, you may want to record the date on which you completed it.

**Romans** ~~1~~ ~~2~~ ~~3~~ ~~4~~ ~~5~~ ~~6~~ ~~7~~ ~~8~~ ~~9~~ ~~10~~ ~~11~~ ~~12~~ ~~13~~ ~~14~~ **15 16** *May 25, 20XX*

For the sake of continuity, we suggest that you read one book completely through before selecting another rather than using the "grasshopper" approach—that is, jumping from passage to passage or from book to book. But sometimes you may enjoy reading an Old Testament and a New Testament book concurrently. For easy access, it is helpful to keep your *My Reading Progress* page in the Bible you use for reading.

**ASSIGNMENT FOR SESSION 4**

1. Scripture Memory: Memorize the verse on "Assurance of Victory," 1 Corinthians 10:13, and work at consistently reviewing your first two memory verses aloud.
2. Bible Reading: Continue your Bible reading and marking. Begin using *My Reading Progress* in conjunction with your Bible reading.
3. Bible Study: Complete the Bible study "Prayer: Part 2" (pages 45–49).
4. Other: Read and mark The Wheel Illustration (pages 49–53).

# SESSION 4

**OUTLINE OF THIS SESSION**

1. Open the session in prayer.
2. Break into groups of two or three and review your memory verses:
   a. "Assurance of Salvation" (1 John 5:11-12)
   b. "Assurance of Answered Prayer" (John 16:24)
   c. "Assurance of Victory" (1 Corinthians 10:13)
3. Share with the rest of the group something you have read and marked in your Bible this week.
4. Discuss "Prayer: Part 2" (pages 45–49).
5. Discuss The Wheel Illustration (pages 49–53).
6. Discuss how to use *My Completion Record* (page 7).
7. Read "Assignment for Session 5" (page 53).
8. Close the session in prayer.

## PRAYER: PART 2 (continued from page 42)

(continued from page 42)

5. Consider Christ's pattern for prayer in Matthew 6:9-13.
   a. How does the prayer begin? Why is this important?

   _____

   _____

   b. Which requests are God-centered? _____

   _____

   _____

   c. Which requests are person-centered? _____

   _____

   _____

   _____

d. In what specific ways can this pattern for praying help you pray?

_____

_____

_____

6. From the following verses, list some of the categories of people for whom we should pray.

Romans 10:1 _____

1 Timothy 2:1-4 _____

Matthew 9:37-38 _____

7. Using Paul's prayer as a guideline, list some requests you could pray for

others and for yourself (Ephesians 3:14-21). _____

_____

_____

_____

_____

_____

_____

_____

_____

_____

Take a moment right now to use these requests to pray for someone you know. Write down the name of the person for whom you prayed.

_____

> We should pray when we are in a praying mood, for it would
> be sinful to neglect so fair an opportunity. We should pray
> when we are not in a proper mood, for it would be
> dangerous to remain in so unhealthy a condition.
> —CHARLES H. SPURGEON

Have you been using a prayer list? A list can help you remember things you might otherwise forget to pray about. It can include:

- Your family
- Your non-Christian friends and acquaintances
- Missionaries and Christian workers you know
- Those who oppose you
- Your pastor and church
- Government authorities
- For more Christian workers
- Your personal needs

8. Paul reveals a powerful key to freedom from worry and anxiety in Philippians 4:6-7.

   a. What are you to do? _____
   
   _____

   b. What is God's promise? _____
   
   _____
   
   _____

   c. In what areas can you immediately begin to apply these truths?
   
   _____
   
   _____
   
   _____

   > It is impossible for a believer, no matter what his experience, to keep right with God if he will not take the trouble to spend time with God. . . . Spend plenty of time with God; let other things go, but don't neglect Him.
   >
   > —OSWALD CHAMBERS

9. Examine Luke 10:38-42. We can make several observations from this passage that relate to our spending time with Jesus Christ.
   a. Contrast the activities of Mary and Martha.

   | MARY | MARTHA |
   | --- | --- |
   | | |
   | | |
   | | |

_____    _____

_____    _____

_____    _____

b. Which one did Jesus commend and why? _____

_____

c. Like Martha, we may be easily distracted by many things. What activities might distract you from listening to and conversing with

God? _____

_____

_____

_____

d. What can you do to overcome these distractions? _____

_____

_____

10. Why was God disappointed with some of His Old Testament followers

(Jeremiah 2:32)? _____

_____

What else impresses you in this verse? _____

_____

_____

_____

Thou are coming to a King;
　　Large petitions with thee bring;
For His grace and power are such,
　　None can ever ask too much!

—JOHN NEWTON

### SUMMARY

God has provided prayer as the way to communicate directly with Him. Christ, the great High Priest and Mediator, has made it possible for all Christians to "approach the throne of grace with confidence" (Hebrews 4:16). Prayer may take many forms of expression, some of which are adoration and praise, thanksgiving, confession, intercession, and supplication. Each of these enables us to draw closer to God. Because we have the potential of two-way communication with God, we will not want to neglect consistent times with Him. Certainly He looks forward to our honest personal conversations with Him.

## THE WHEEL ILLUSTRATION

The Wheel Illustration depicts six of the crucially important components of a vital Christian life. Your Bible studies in this course (book 1) cover each of these six topics. In book 2, you will memorize verses on these six topics.

Three important dimensions of The Wheel are:

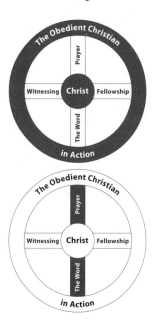

1. The Volitional Dimension
   (Your Relationship to Your Will)
   The Hub: Christ the Center
   The Rim: Obedience to Christ

2. The Vertical Dimension
   (Your Relationship to God)
   The Word Spoke
   The Prayer Spoke

3. The Horizontal Dimension
(Your relationship to Others)
The Fellowship Spoke
The Witnessing Spoke

## THE VOLITIONAL DIMENSION

(YOUR RELATIONSHIP TO YOUR WILL)

### The Hub: Christ the Center

The act of making Christ central in your life—that is, giving Him the place of true lordship in your life—is really an act of your will. It is a decision that you make, and there may be times of recommitment. There should be a moment in your life when you are willing to surrender totally to Christ's authority and lordship. This may be as a new Christian or after some months or even years.

It is true that lordship is a volitional matter—that is, a matter of your choice or your will. But as you pray and as others pray for you, God creates within you the desire to do what He wants you to do in order to express His lordship in your life.

> For it is God who works in you to will and to act according
> to his good purpose.
>
> —PHILIPPIANS 2:13

### The Rim: Obedience to Christ

When you are obedient to Christ and actively follow God's leading, it will show in your outward lifestyle. People can see the evidences of your Christianity.

Some acts of obedience to God are more internal. They have to do with attitudes, habits, motives, sense of values, and day-to-day thoughts. These internal acts of obedience eventually surface in relationships with other people. The proof of your love for God is your demonstrated obedience to Him.

> But I gave them this command: Obey me, and I will be your
> God and you will be my people. Walk in all the ways I
> command you, that it may go well with you.
>
> —JEREMIAH 7:23

## THE VERTICAL DIMENSION
(YOUR RELATIONSHIP TO GOD)

### The Word Spoke

In this illustration, "the Word" is the foundational spoke. In practice, this spoke is perhaps the most crucial element in a balanced Christian life. Through the Bible, God shows us His principles for life and ministry. We learn to obey, and we increasingly see Christ as worthy of our unqualified allegiance.

As you have a vital personal intake of the Word of God, you stay healthy and continue growing.

> All scripture is inspired by God and is useful for teaching the faith and correcting error, for re-setting the direction of a man's life and training him in good living. The scriptures are the comprehensive equipment of the man of God, and fit him fully for all branches of his work.
>
> —2 TIMOTHY 3:16-17 (PH)

### The Prayer Spoke

Prayer is the natural overflow of meaningful time in the Bible. Our talking to God completes the fellowship element in our relationship with Him. We respond back to God in prayer after He speaks to us through His Word. We are sharing our heart with the One who longs for our companionship.

Prayer can unleash the power of God. Personal battles for others can be won through prayer, and the cause of Christ can be furthered in the world!

> Call to Me, and I will answer you, and show you great and mighty things which you do not know.
>
> —JEREMIAH 33:3 (NKJV)

> You do not have, because you do not ask God.
>
> —JAMES 4:2

## THE HORIZONTAL DIMENSION
(YOUR RELATIONSHIP TO OTHERS)

### *The Fellowship Spoke*

Christians are neither higher nor lower than other people. Someone has said that "the ground is level at the foot of the cross." We have the privilege of close, meaningful interaction with other members of God's family.

We can learn from one another and spread encouragement. Among like-minded believers, we experience a dynamic, spiritual reinforcement. This doesn't happen if we operate independently in isolation from other Christians.

> From him the whole body, joined and held together by every supporting ligament, grows and builds itself up in love, as each part does its work.
>
> —EPHESIANS 4:16

### *The Witnessing Spoke*

When a person has a vibrant life in Christ, it is natural to want to explain to others how they can also have it. Your devotional life, extended times of prayer, and prompt obedience to God will give your life an attractiveness that draws people and adds credibility to your words.

Effective witnessing also involves skills. Skills can be developed. We can become a sharpened instrument in God's hand as we get training and experience.

> But you will receive power when the Holy Spirit comes on you; and you will be my witnesses in Jerusalem, and in all Judea and Samaria, and to the ends of the earth.
>
> —ACTS 1:8

### THE COMPOSITE (THE WHEEL AS A WHOLE)

Usually "either/or" thinking is not reliable. Most of life is "both/and." It is not *either* fellowship *or* witnessing; it is not *either* prayer *or* an intake of the Word. A balanced Christian life includes several ingredients. It is the wise believer who intentionally pursues balance.

Develop your strengths and trust God to use them to the fullest extent. Also work on your deficiencies and inadequacies, trusting the Holy Spirit to continue to renovate you.

The Wheel is a good checklist for evaluating growth and balance in your spiritual life. Over the months and years, you want to see a continual development and strengthening of your spiritual life in a number of areas.

> All the believers devoted themselves to the apostles' teaching, and to fellowship, and to sharing in meals (including the Lord's Supper), and to prayer . . . all the while praising God and enjoying the goodwill of all the people. And each day the Lord added to their fellowship those who were being saved.
>
> —ACTS 2:42,47 (NLT)

**ASSIGNMENT FOR SESSION 5**

1. Scripture Memory: No new memory verses are assigned for next session. Polish up the three passages you know. You will find it a great help if you review each of your learned verses at least once a day.
2. Bible Reading: Continue your Bible reading and marking. Continue using *My Reading Progress* along with your Bible reading.
   a. Read and mark "How to Use *My Reading Highlights*" (pages 59–60).
   b. Read and mark "Why Use *My Reading Highlights*" (pages 60–61).
3. Bible Study: Complete the Bible study "The Word" (pages 61–66).
4. Other: Read "Practical Suggestions on Prayer" (pages 55–59) and complete questions 1a, 1b, 1c, 4, and 5. The rest will be done in class. You can locate copies of *My Reading Highlights* in the appendix (pages 123–152) or online at www.2-7series.org.

# SESSION 5

**OUTLINE OF THIS SESSION**

1. Open the session in prayer.
2. Break into groups of two or three and review your memory verses:
   a. "Assurance of Salvation" (1 John 5:11-12)
   b. "Assurance of Answered Prayer" (John 16:24)
   c. "Assurance of Victory" (1 Corinthians 10:13)
3. Share with your group something you have read and marked in your Bible this week.
4. Complete and discuss "Practical Suggestions on Prayer" (pages 55–59).
5. Discuss the how and why of using *My Reading Highlights* (pages 59–61).
6. Discuss the Bible study "The Word" (pages 61–66).
7. Read "Assignment for Session 6" (page 67).
8. Close the session in prayer.

## PRACTICAL SUGGESTIONS ON PRAYER

**THINK ABOUT:**

Prayer is not an attempt to change God's mind; real prayer is communion with God. By it we express our trust in Him, seek to know His mind on the decisions of life, submit to His will, resist in His name the efforts of the Devil to frustrate God's loving purposes in human lives.

—LEITH SAMUEL

1. Prayer: an indispensable part of fellowship with God.
   a. What do these two verses say about our fellowship with God?

   1 Corinthians 1:9 _____

   _____

   _____

1 John 1:3 _____

_____

b. What do you think are some keys to having effective fellowship with other people? List single words or short phrases. _____

_____

Many of the same ingredients between people are essential for fellowship and communication between a person and God.

c. From your answers in question b, list two ingredients you feel are very important to fellowship and communication between a person and God.

_____

_____

d. What are the fewest elements you can have and still have fellowship with someone?

They talk to me as I _____ and I _____ to them as they listen.

This applies to our relationship with God as well. God "talks" to us through our daily reading in the Bible, and we talk to God by praying.

2. An example of POOR COMMUNICATION with God.

The following diagram illustrates poor and ineffective communication with God during Bible reading and marking.

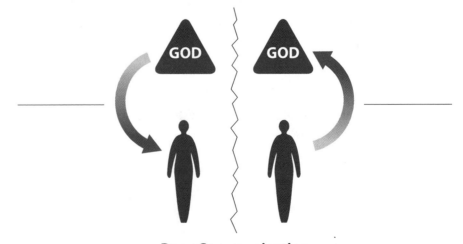

**Poor Communication**

On the left, we see the Christian listening as God speaks to him or her through the Bible. Then on the right, we see the Christian praying after completing a time of Bible reading. But the topics of the prayer are unrelated to what God has just "said" to the reader. We would not be so rude as to ignore the comments of a human friend, immediately jumping in with what we want to say, yet we sometimes inadvertently do this to God. This is poor communication.

3. An example of EFFECTIVE COMMUNICATION with God.

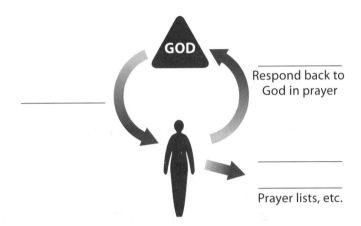

Respond back to God in prayer

Prayer lists, etc.

**Effective Communication**

The element that makes this second approach so meaningful and effective is our responding back to God in prayer. Here are two ways you might do that:

a. Comment back to God each time you mark something in your Bible.

b. Complete your reading and marking, and then go back to make a brief prayer comment about one or more things you marked. Whether you choose "a" or "b," you might respond by:

- Thanking God for something, or praising Him
- Asking God for help in applying something you just read
- Talking to Him about something the Bible passage brought to mind

God relishes your sincere heart response to what He has privately "said" to you during your reading. You want to leave "Other Prayers" for last. You can focus on those prayers after finishing your reading and responding back to God in prayer.

4. There are two sides of prayer: speaking and listening. God primarily speaks to us through Scripture and we speak to God by praying (in our

heart or aloud). But we want to be sensitive to what God might "say" to us while we are close to Him, talking to Him in prayer. As you are reading or praying, listen for impressions or nudges from God in your mind or in your heart. After months of personal time with God through Scripture and in prayer, you become more adept at "hearing" God.

What are your observations about communication with God from the following two passages?

a. David speaking to God: "When You said, 'Seek My face,' my heart said to You, 'Your face, LORD, I will seek'" (Psalm 27:8, NKJV).

_____

_____

_____

_____

b. "Let the morning bring me word of your unfailing love, for I have put my trust in you. Show me the way I should go, for to you I lift up my soul. Rescue me from my enemies, O LORD, for I hide myself in you. Teach me to do your will, for you are my God; may your good Spirit lead me on level ground" (Psalm 143:8-10).

_____

_____

_____

_____

5. How the Trinity is involved in prayer: We pray to the Father, in the name of Jesus Christ, aided by the Holy Spirit. Please take a few moments to read and think about the summary statement and verses under each of the three persons of the Trinity.

a. The Father

Our prayers should be directed primarily to the Father.

[Jesus told His disciples:] This, then, is how you should pray: "Our Father in heaven, hallowed be your name."

— MATTHEW 6:9

[Jesus:] After Jesus said this, he looked toward heaven and prayed: "Father, the time has come. Glorify your Son, that your Son may glorify you."

— JOHN 17:1

[Paul:] For this reason I kneel before the Father.

—Ephesians 3:14

b. The Son, Jesus Christ

We come to the Father on the merits of Jesus Christ—that is, in His name. Christ is our access to the Father.

You did not choose me, but I chose you and appointed you to go and bear fruit—fruit that will last. Then the Father will give you whatever you ask in my name.

—John 15:16

I tell you the truth, my Father will give you whatever you ask in my name. Until now you have not asked for anything in my name. Ask and you will receive, and your joy will be complete.

—John 16:23-24

c. The Holy Spirit

The Holy Spirit gives us guidance in what we should pray and interprets for the Father what is on our hearts, even when our words are poorly framed.

In the same way, the Spirit helps us in our weakness. We do not know what we ought to pray for, but the Spirit himself intercedes for us with groans that words cannot express.

—Romans 8:26

Groanings which cannot be uttered are often prayers which cannot be refused.

—C. H. Spurgeon

## HOW TO USE *MY READING HIGHLIGHTS*

1. Do your daily Bible reading and marking each day.
2. Then leaf back through what you have read and choose the one thought that is most interesting or helpful to you. It does not have to be a profound thought, but it might be what you consider the best thing you marked.
3. At this point, fill in *My Reading Highlights* for that day.

a. **Translation**: record the translation you are reading.

b. **Year**: record the current year.

c. ☐: a place to check off Scripture memory review.

d. **Date**: record the current date.

e. **All I read today**: record the reference(s) for the day's reading. For example: Ezra 2–4 or John 3.

f. **Best thing I marked today**: put in the reference and then copy the verse or part of the verse that impressed you. (Paraphrase it if you like, but that takes more time.) For example:

Best thing I marked today: Reference: *Acts 6:7*

Thought: *"The word of God spread. The number of disciples in Jerusalem increased rapidly, and a large number of priests became obedient to the faith."*

g. **How it impressed me**: write down what the phrase, sentence, or passage meant to you. Here's an example based on Acts 6:7.

How it impressed me: *I want to be a person growing in my ability to effectively present the gospel—I want to spread it! I also want to become a strong disciple and learn how to help other Christians become strong disciples. I want to be a 100 percenter, by God's grace!*

4. Write legibly. You might be surprised how often you will come back to entries in *My Reading Highlights*.

5. If you prefer, write your entries in a spiral notebook or blank journal book, or record them digitally. For now, keep your entries about the same length as the space provided on *My Reading Highlights*.

## WHY USE *MY READING HIGHLIGHTS*

1. **It gives you one thought to reflect on each day**. Let's say you are impressed with an average of five things in your reading each day. If you isolate the best of the five, it gives you one thing to think about between readings. This allows God to use what He has been impressing on your mind to change your life. Focus your thinking on that one idea during the day, giving God the opportunity to enrich your life as a result of your reading.

2. **It may help you see trends in God's dealing with you**. With a record of

major things God has been saying to you over a period of days or weeks, it is often possible to identify a pattern. This may help you better understand your past and your present, and it could help your thinking about the future.

3. **It gives you something specific to share with others**. Often if you are asked to give a devotional, teach a class, or deliver a message, this material can be expanded or combined. It has vitality because God has spoken to you personally. You may also find opportunities to use these devotional thoughts to encourage or challenge others.

4. **It helps to sharpen and organize your mind**. Learning to sift through your reading to determine what is most important will sharpen your mind to do the same thing in other areas such as job, school, family decisions, and counseling others.

5. **It stimulates consistency in your reading**. You may find, as others have, that writing out a thought each day increases your consistency in reading. You are also less likely to miss a day when you realize that there will be a blank space left on *My Reading Highlights*. There are stronger motivators, but this subtle prod helps us all. For strong results, plan to read at least five out of the seven days during a week; six or seven days benefit you even more.

# THE WORD

**THINK ABOUT:**

How would you respond to a skeptic's statement that the Bible is merely a book written by people and is no different from any other book?

The Bible is the most remarkable book ever written. The writing was done by about forty authors from several countries and many occupations. They wrote over a period of approximately 1,500 years and in three languages (Hebrew, Aramaic, and Greek). Yet the Bible has one great theme and central figure: Jesus Christ. All of this would be impossible unless the Bible had one supreme Author—and it does—the Holy Spirit of God.

**GOD'S WORD: INSPIRED—RELIABLE—SUFFICIENT**

1. How do the writers of Old Testament Scriptures attribute their words to God in the following passages?

Nehemiah 9:13-14 _____

2 Samuel 23:1-3 _____

Jeremiah 1:6-9 _____

2. What conclusions about the reliability of Scripture can you draw from the following New Testament passages?

1 Thessalonians 2:13 _____

2 Peter 1:20-21 _____

2 Peter 3:15-16 _____

*Inspired* comes from the Greek word meaning "God-breathed."

> The meaning, then, is not that God breathed into the writers, nor that He somehow breathed into the writings to give them their special character, but that what was written by men was breathed out by God. He spoke through them. They were his spokesmen.
>
> —JOHN R. W. STOTT

3. How did Jesus use Scripture in the following situations?
   a. In explaining the difference between true and false worship (Mark 7:6-9).

   _____

   _____

   _____

   b. In answering a tough question about the resurrection (Mark 12:24-27).

   _____

   _____

   c. In avoiding an argument with an insincere questioner (Luke 10:25-28).

   _____

   _____

   _____

d. Jesus relied on God's Word for His life and ministry. Based on your answers to the last three questions, what one or two principles can you draw from Jesus' use of Scripture?

_____

_____

_____

_____

4. Second Timothy 3:16-17 is an excellent summary statement of the inspiration and sufficiency of God's Word.

a. From verse 16, list and define four ways that Scripture is of value to us.

1. _____      _____

                      _____

2. _____      _____

                      _____

3. _____      _____

                      _____

4. _____      _____

                      _____

b. What is one major result of the Scriptures' impacting our life (verse 17)?

_____

_____

## GOD'S WORD IN YOUR LIFE

A sword is designed to be used skillfully in battle both as an offensive and defensive weapon. God has equipped you with a tremendous instrument for spiritual battle: "the sword of the Spirit, which is the word of God" (Ephesians 6:17). The Holy Spirit uses the Word of God to accomplish the work of God.

5. Examine Psalm 19:7-8. In the Old Testament, there are synonyms for the Bible (ordinances, decrees, promises, and so on). According to these two verses, please list the synonym (title) used, a characteristic, and how it can benefit you.

| VERSE | SYNONYM | CHARACTERISTIC | HOW IT BENEFITS ME |
|-------|---------|----------------|--------------------|
| 7a | | | |

# The Bible at a Glance  66 books

## Old Testament  39 books

**History**
17 books

**Law**
1. Genesis
2. Exodus
3. Leviticus
4. Numbers
5. Deuteronomy

**History and Government**
1. Joshua
2. Judges
3. Ruth
4. 1 Samuel
5. 2 Samuel
6. 1 Kings
7. 2 Kings
8. 1 Chronicles
9. 2 Chronicles
10. Ezra
11. Nehemiah
12. Esther

**Poetry**
5 books

1. Job
2. Psalms
3. Proverbs
4. Ecclesiastes
5. Song of Solomon

**Prophecy**
17 books

**Major Prophets**
1. Isaiah
2. Jeremiah
3. Lamentations
4. Ezekiel
5. Daniel

**Minor Prophets**
1. Hosea
2. Joel
3. Amos
4. Obadiah
5. Jonah
6. Micah
7. Nahum
8. Habakkuk
9. Zephaniah
10. Haggai
11. Zechariah
12. Malachi

"The New is in the Old concealed. The Old is in the New revealed."

## New Testament  27 books

**History**
5 books

**Gospels**
1. Matthew
2. Mark
3. Luke
4. John

5. Acts

**Teaching**
21 books

**Paul's Letters**
1. Romans
2. 1 Corinthians
3. 2 Corinthians
4. Galatians
5. Ephesians
6. Philippians
7. Colossians
8. 1 Thessalonians
9. 2 Thessalonians
10. 1 Timothy
11. 2 Timothy
12. Titus
13. Philemon

**General Letters**
1. Hebrews
2. James
3. 1 Peter
4. 2 Peter
5. 1 John
6. 2 John
7. 3 John
8. Jude

**Prophecy**
1 book

Revelation

---

The Old Testament looks forward to Christ's sacrifice on the cross.

About 400 years between Testaments

The New Testament is based on the work Christ finished on the cross.

---

God used 40 different men over a period of 1,500 years (about 1400 BC to AD 90) in writing the Bible—2 Peter 1:20-21

7b  _____  _____  _____

8a  _____  _____  _____

8b  _____  _____  _____

Which of the above characteristics is most important to you? Why?

_____

_____

_____

6. Analogy is a form that explains something by comparing it point by
   point with something similar. In the following verses, with what is God's
   Word (the Bible) compared? What function can each of these objects
   perform?

|  | **OBJECT** | **FUNCTION** |
|---|---|---|
| Jeremiah 23:29 | | |
| Matthew 4:4 | | |
| James 1:23-25 | | |

7. Ezra is a good example of someone who felt a responsibility toward God's
   Word. What was his approach to Scripture (Ezra 7:10)?

_____

_____

_____

_____

_____

8. From Joshua 1:8, briefly state the relationships between meditation,
   application, and success.

_____

_____

_____

_____

_____

_____

9. How would you define meditation?

_____

_____

_____

10. Using the material discussed in this chapter, briefly describe one important concept concerning God's Word.

_____

_____

_____

How might you incorporate this into your life to a greater degree?

_____

_____

_____

## SUMMARY

God has communicated to men and women through His Word, the Bible. The Bible is the final authority in all matters of faith and conduct. Through Scripture, we can get to know God better, understand His desire for our lives, and discover new truths about living for Him. God asks believers to let His Word dwell richly in them (Colossians 3:16), so it is important to give ourselves wholeheartedly to allowing God's Word to fill our lives. God places great emphasis on the act of meditating on His Word, which leads to understanding and personal application. Meditation and application not only help us get deeper into the Bible but also allow the Bible teachings to permeate our daily lifestyle.

> The Bible was not given to increase our knowledge but to change our lives.
>
> —D. L. MOODY

> Other books were given for our information; the Bible was given for our transformation.
>
> —UNKNOWN

**ASSIGNMENT FOR SESSION 6**

1. Scripture Memory: Memorize the verse on "Assurance of Forgiveness," 1 John 1:9.
2. Bible Reading: Continue your Bible reading and marking.
3. Other:
   a. Fill in "The Quiet Time" (pages 71–72) by writing a summary for each of the eight verses.
   b. Read and mark "Quiet Time, Reading Plans, and Bible Study" (pages 72–74).

# SESSION 6

**OUTLINE OF THIS SESSION**

1. Open the session in prayer.
2. Break into groups of two or three and review your memory verses:
   a. "Assurance of Salvation" (1 John 5:11-12)
   b. "Assurance of Answered Prayer" (John 16:24)
   c. "Assurance of Victory" (1 Corinthians 10:13)
   d. "Assurance of Forgiveness (1 John 1:9)
3. Share with the rest of your group something you have read and marked in your Bible this week.
4. Discuss The Hand Illustration (pages 69–71).
5. Discuss "The Quiet Time" (pages 71–72).
6. Discuss "Quiet Time, Reading Plans, and Bible Study" (pages 72–74).
7. Read "Assignment for Session 7" (page 74).
8. Close the session in prayer.

## THE HAND ILLUSTRATION

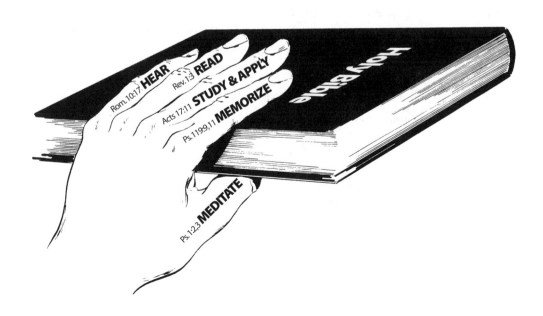

The Hand Illustration shows us how to have a practical, working grasp on the Bible. It has been estimated that we remember:

- 5 percent of what we HEAR
- 15 percent of what we READ
- 35 percent of what we STUDY
- 100 percent of what we MEMORIZE

So a balanced intake of the Bible comes through hearing, reading, studying, and memorizing. Then as we meditate on Scripture during these four activities, the Bible content touches our lives in a more personal and specific way, helping us grow spiritually and become more like Christ.

Let us look in more detail at these five methods of learning from the Bible.

1. **Hearing** the Word of God from godly pastors and teachers provides us with insight from Bible study done by others. It also stimulates our own appetite for Scripture. (Taking notes can increase our ability to retain what we hear.)

   Consequently, faith comes from hearing the message, and the message is heard through the word of Christ. (Romans 10:17)

2. **Reading** the Bible gives us an overall picture of Scripture and is also the foundation of the daily quiet time.

   Blessed is the one who reads the words of this prophecy, and blessed are those who hear it and take to heart what is written in it, because the time is near. (Revelation 1:3)

3. **Studying** the Bible is more in-depth than reading. It leads us to sound doctrine and personal convictions about the major teachings of Scripture.

   Now the Bereans were of more noble character than the Thessalonians, for they received the message with great eagerness and examined the Scriptures every day to see if what Paul said was true. (Acts 17:11)

4. **Memorizing** God's Word prepares us to use the Sword of the Spirit to overcome temptation and provides verses at our fingertips for helping and encouraging others.

How can a young man keep his way pure? By living according to your word. I seek you with all my heart; do not let me stray from your commands. I have hidden your word in my heart that I might not sin against you. (Psalm 119:9-11)

5. **Meditation** enhances the effectiveness of the other four methods of Scripture intake. Only as we meditate on God's Word (thinking of its meaning and application to our lives) will we discover its transforming power in our lives.

But his delight is in the law of the LORD, and on his law he meditates day and night. He is like a tree planted by streams of water, which yields its fruit in season and whose leaf does not wither. (Psalm 1:2-3)

## THE QUIET TIME

1. What is a quiet time?
   a. It is an unhurried time of meeting with God through Bible reading and prayer.
   b. It is at the heart of our fellowship with God.

   The men who have most fully illustrated Christ in their characters, and have most powerfully affected the world for Him, have been men who spend so much time with God as to make it a notable feature in their lives. . . . To be little with God is to be little for God.
   —E. M. BOUNDS

2. There are two major reasons for having a quiet time: for growth and nourishment and for intimacy with God. Let's look at both.
   a. For growth and nourishment
      Food and proper nutrition are essential to healthy physical growth. In the same way, consistent intake of God's Word causes Christian growth and good spiritual health. Summarize what the following verses say about spiritual growth and nourishment.

1 Peter 2:2 _____

Psalm 119:103 _____

Jeremiah 15:16 _____

Hebrews 5:12-14 _____

b. For vital companionship with God

   Summarize what the following verses say about intimacy with our triune God.

Psalm 16:11 _____

Micah 6:8 _____

John 15:4 _____

1 Corinthians 1:9 _____

That we ought to act with God in the greatest simplicity, speaking to Him frankly and plainly, and imploring His assistance in our affairs, just as they happen.

—BROTHER LAWRENCE

## QUIET TIME, READING PLANS, AND BIBLE STUDY

There are several differences between Bible reading done during quiet time and Bible reading done as part of a structured reading plan. Bible study serves yet another purpose. Here we look at all three.

## 1. BIBLE READING

### A. QUIET-TIME READING

*The Mindset*

In the quiet time approach used in this course, you read and mark only a chapter or two each day. You do not hurry. We are meeting a Person, not a habit or routine. We expect God to impress us with something we need to hear from the Bible that day. Looking back over several weeks, you might observe a pattern or emphasis. God may be repeating something He wants you to apply or understand.

As you read, look for the overall theme of a chapter or book. Quiet-time reading sharpens your familiarity with people and events from both the Old and New Testaments.

Reading is like flying over a city in an airplane or helicopter or viewing a broad computer satellite image of a city. We see the general landscape (parks, lakes, major buildings, and other landmarks), but we miss much of the detail. (It is in Bible study that we discover the details of Scripture.)

### The Pattern

In the quiet time, you are READING, MARKING, RESPONDING back to God in prayer, and RECORDING something that catches your eye. Your quiet time can be fun, refreshing, and uplifting. Mark what interests you. Enjoy yourself.

### The Goals

One major benefit of quiet-time reading is Christian growth. As we read Bible passages with an open heart, those verses can have a purifying influence on our thoughts, desires, and motivations. Bible reading helps us experience Paul's advice in Romans 12:2: "Do not conform any longer to the pattern of this world, but be transformed by the renewing of your mind."

### B. READING PLANS

*More Time, Less Personal*

A printed or online Bible reading plan is usually structured to help you read through the Bible in one calendar year. It might include charts and commentary—helpful, but time-consuming. Most people find reading plans less personal with God than a quiet-time approach.

### C. HAVING BOTH A QUIET TIME AND A READING PLAN

*Cut Back or Reorganize*

What if you are committed to a reading plan? You may find it best to discontinue the reading plan while you are in THE 2:7 SERIES. But if you have discretionary time, you might, for example, choose to do your daily quiet time in the morning and the reading plan in the evening. Don't overload yourself. You want to follow a schedule that keeps reading enjoyable for you.

## 2. BIBLE STUDY

We compared reading to an aerial view of a city. Bible study is like driving through the city: learning street names and locating the supermarket, bank, and shopping mall. More and more, we feel at home in the city. Bible study allows you to dig deeper into the awesome teachings of Scripture. You sense that it is deepening your convictions and helping you apply specific principles and guidelines to your everyday life. Bible study is more time-consuming than reading. We may thoughtfully read through a chapter in two to five minutes, but to study the chapter may take an hour or more.

Bible reading and Bible study each play a distinctive role in sharpening and deepening your Christian life and give you things to share with others.

**ASSIGNMENT FOR SESSION 7**

1. Scripture Memory: If you are caught up on your other Scripture memory, you might work ahead on Proverbs 3:5-6 and John 5:24. Continue to review your four *Beginning with Christ* verses at least once a day, if possible.

2. Quiet Time: Continue your Bible reading and marking. Pick a highlight from your reading each day and record it on *My Reading Highlights*. Please bring *My Reading Highlights* with you next week so you can share something from it.

3. Bible Study: Complete the Bible study "Christ the Center" (pages 75–80).

# SESSION 7

OUTLINE OF THIS SESSION

1. Open the session in prayer.
2. Break into groups of two or three and review your first four *Beginning with Christ* memory verses. Get items signed off on *My Completion Record*.
3. Share at least one item from *My Reading Highlights* with your group.
4. Discuss the Bible study "Christ the Center" (pages 75–80).
5. Read "Assignment for Session 8" (page 80).
6. Close the session in prayer.

## CHRIST THE CENTER

Jesus Christ is Savior and Lord!

William Barclay has pointed out that "of all the titles of Jesus, the title Lord became by far the most commonly used, widespread, and theologically important. It would hardly be going too far to say that the word Lord became a synonym for the name Jesus."[2] This sometimes-neglected aspect of the Christian experience needs to be carefully considered by all men and women who want to live as His disciples.

---

**THINK ABOUT:**

What are some indicators of what is central in someone's life?

_____

_____

_____

---

THE LORD JESUS CHRIST

1. Titles reveal important information about the person to whom they refer. What are Jesus Christ's titles in the following verses?

John 13:13 _____

Acts 2:36 _____

Revelation 19:16 _____

Summarize what these titles reveal about Jesus Christ. _____

_____

_____

2. List some of the things you learn about Christ from Colossians 1:15-20.

_____

_____

_____

_____

_____

In light of who Christ is, what position has the Father given Him (verse 18)? _____

_____

_____

> Christ should have the same place in our hearts that He holds in the universe.
>
> —UNKNOWN

3. Examine Philippians 2:9-11.

a. How has God exalted Jesus Christ? _____

_____

_____

b. How will every person exalt Him? _____

_____

_____

4. Read 1 Corinthians 6:19-20.

a. How did you become God's possession? _____

_____

b. Therefore, what should you do? _____

_____

Jesus Christ, Lord of lords, has always existed and always will. Not all people allow Him to be the center of their lives, but that does not alter the fact of His lordship. All will someday acknowledge Christ as Lord, but right now, in our daily living we have the opportunity to acknowledge His lordship. We can allow Him to become the center of our lives. Allow Christ to be the Lord of your life through a decision followed by daily practice.

## ACKNOWLEDGING HIS LORDSHIP

5. What are we urged to do in Romans 12:1? _____

_____

_____

_____

_____

Why should we do this? _____

_____

_____

> Christ is present in all Christians;
> Christ is prominent in some Christians;
> But in only a few Christians is Christ preeminent.
>
> — UNKNOWN

6. There are many reasons people are reluctant to give Christ access to every area of their lives. Check any of the following sentences that apply to you.
   a. I generally think or feel that:

   _____ Jesus doesn't really understand my problems.

   _____ He may want me to do something I can't.

   _____ He may lead me into a career I will dislike.

   _____ He will prevent me from getting married.

   _____ He will take away my enjoyment of possessions, hobbies, or friends.

   _____ He can help me in the "big" things, but He doesn't care about the little things.

b. Are there any other fears that have prevented you from giving Christ access to every area of your life?

_____

_____

c. How does the statement in Jeremiah 29:11 dispel these fears?

_____

_____

> The passion of Christianity comes from deliberately signing away my own rights and becoming a bond-servant of Jesus Christ. Until I do that, I will not begin to be a saint.
>
> —OSWALD CHAMBERS

7. Good intentions don't guarantee good results. A good start does not ensure a strong finish—deciding is only the beginning. One business person said, "Success is 10 percent decision and 90 percent follow-through." Once we have acknowledged the lordship of Christ in our lives, we prove that He is Lord by submitting to Him hour by hour and obeying Him in the daily affairs of life. Some of these areas are represented in the following illustration.

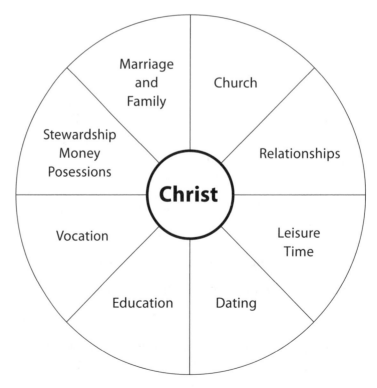

8. Take a few moments to evaluate your practice of the lordship of Jesus Christ.

a. Over which of the preceding areas would you currently like to see Christ have more control? _____

_____

b. What are some specific changes you would like to see Christ help you make in these areas? _____

_____

We don't want to be concerned about what we would do for the Lord if we only had more money, time, or education. Instead, we should decide how to manage the resources and circumstances we have now. What matters is whether or not we are allowing Christ to control us.

> God being who and what He is, and we being who and what we are, the only thinkable relation between us is one of full lordship on His part and complete submission on ours. We owe Him every honor that is in our power to give Him.
>
> —A. W. Tozer

9. What three things is the person who decides to follow Christ called to do (Luke 9:23)?

The action to take: _____

What this means in my own words: _____

_____

The action to take: _____

What this means in my own words: _____

_____

The action to take: _____

What this means in my own words: _____

_____

10. According to Luke 6:46, what is a good way to evaluate if Christ is truly Lord of your life? _____

_____

_____

11. What does making Christ the center of your life mean to you personally?

_____

_____

_____

_____

_____

**SUMMARY**

In the Bible, Jesus Christ is declared to be Lord. He is worthy of that role because of who He is and not merely because of what He has done.

Although Christ is Lord, He does not hold a preeminent place in the heart of every believer. Some areas of a Christian's life might not yet be subject to the control of Christ. We want to increasingly turn over more areas of our lives to Christ. As He becomes the Leader of our lives, we experience fulfillment and joy.

**ASSIGNMENT FOR SESSION 8**

1. Scripture Memory: Memorize the passage on "Assurance of Guidance," Proverbs 3:5-6.
2. Quiet Time: Continue reading and marking in your Bible and using *My Reading Highlights*.
3. Other:
   a. Study and be ready to discuss the material from "Guide to Conversational Prayer" (pages 84–85).
   b. We will read the evangelism suggestions in class (pages 81–82).
   c. Complete "The Wheel and The Hand in Your Life" (page 83). Please leave question 4 blank in both sections.
   d. Review all previous sessions when you can block out some time to leaf through all seven sessions and give some thought to each page. Come prepared to share what has impressed, helped, or challenged you during this course.
   e. Work on getting everything you can completed and ready to be signed off on *My Completion Record*.

# SESSION 8

OUTLINE OF THIS SESSION

1. Open the session in prayer.
2. Break into groups of two or three and review all five *Beginning with Christ* verses.
3. Share some highlights from your reading, particularly those you have recorded on *My Reading Highlights*.
4. Share what has impressed, helped, or challenged you during this course.
5. Read and discuss the evangelism suggestions found on pages 81–82.
6. Discuss "The Wheel and The Hand in Your Life" (page 83).
7. Discuss "Guide to Conversational Prayer" (pages 84–85).
8. Read "Assignment for Session 9" (page 85).
9. Have a brief time of conversational prayer on two or three topics.

## WHY HAVE AN EVANGELISM PRAYER LIST

One of the most exciting events that can happen to you as a Christian is to see someone you know come to a saving knowledge of the Lord Jesus Christ. The situation that would make a person's conversion even more thrilling would be if you had been praying for that person.

In his book *Winning Ways*, LeRoy Eims makes the following statement: "If you want to see particular persons won to Christ, I suggest you put their names on a prayer list. Then pray for opportunities to share the gospel with them, ask God to prepare their hearts, and pray until God gives the promised answer."[3] The apostle Paul expressed his concern for his fellow Israelites in his letter to the Romans: "Brothers, my heart's desire and prayer to God for the Israelites is that they may be saved" (Romans 10:1).

A key to seeing people come to Christ is to keep them on your mind and be specifically praying for them. An evangelism prayer list helps you do this.

# SETTING UP YOUR EVANGELISM PRAYER LIST

We want people around us to become committed followers of Jesus Christ. Our first step is to identify friends around us who need Christ. Then we can begin to pray for them regularly. Prayer is where major victories are won.

1. Pray for wisdom in establishing your prayer list.
2. List the names of between five and ten non-Christians with whom you have contact. These could be neighbors, relatives, people at work, friends from school, and others. You can add other names to the list later as more people come to mind.
3. You can use an index card to list these people and carry it in your reading Bible as a marker. As you begin to pray regularly for these people, look for ways to develop a stronger friendship with them. Pray about where and how they might clearly hear the gospel.

## GETTING TO KNOW NON-CHRISTIANS

Many Christians find they have very few non-Christian friends. Here are suggestions for knowing and relating to more people. (We are not manipulating people; we are taking an interest in them and caring about their situations, men with men and women with women.)

1. **Get to know people at work or at school**. Take the initiative to meet people. Welcome new neighbors, be outside when your neighbors are; attend children's school activities, participate in homeowners association events, and so on.
2. **Enjoy doing things with one or several of them**. Work out with them, give some time to a hobby, or participate in sports together.
3. **Be friendly and sociable**. Ask God to help you develop the kind of rapport and friendship where (when the opportunity presents itself) you can share the gospel in a genuinely caring and personal way. Social and fun times together and with others become intermediate steps toward people coming to Christ.

# THE WHEEL AND THE HAND IN YOUR LIFE

Doing this little personal inventory can help each of us make adjustments in our schedules and in our choices of activities. Doing this assessment once or twice a year keeps us sharp. Here goes:

At this point in time, as you look at The Wheel (pages 49–53) and The Hand (pages 69–71), in which area would you say you are strongest in The Wheel and The Hand, and in which area are you the weakest in each?

**THE WHEEL**

1. I feel I am strongest in _____

2. I feel I am weakest in _____

3. What insights or questions do your answers bring to mind? _____

_____

_____

_____

4. Helpful comments from others during the group sharing: _____

_____

_____

_____

**THE HAND**

1. I feel I am strongest in _____

2. I feel I am weakest in _____

3. What insights or questions do your answers bring to mind? _____

_____

_____

_____

4. Helpful comments from others during the group sharing: _____

_____

_____

_____

# GUIDE TO CONVERSATIONAL PRAYER

God desires your fellowship, and you can participate in a new dimension of communication with Him through conversational prayer. This is a type of group prayer. It is informal. The group speaks conversationally with God from their hearts. We don't think about impressing those who hear us. We are less concerned with the wording and structure of our prayers and more interested in sincere, open communication with God.

Here are some guidelines:

1. **Start praying rather than sharing requests**. Much of a group's valuable prayer time can be taken up in sharing requests rather than praying. Usually the person with the burden for someone or something will be the one to initiate prayer about that person or thing. People in the group will know more facts and details about situations than there is time to pray. So in your mind, choose one or two things to pray.

2. **Pray about one topic at a time**. It is helpful to pray topically as much as possible. One person may pray about a sick friend, and the second person can stay on that topic by asking for strength for the family while the sick relative recuperates. Then another may pray that the family's financial needs be met during this lengthy illness. When there is a pause, someone might change the topic. For example, after a pause, a person might pray for help in having consistent quiet times. Another may request that his quiet time be more meaningful. Another prays that she will have the time to meditate on the Scripture she reads during her quiet time. You want to keep from skipping around from topic to topic. You don't want a disjointed time. You want a meaningful prayer time in which the group members care about each other's prayers. The group is in agreement and praying along silently as each person prays.

3. **Pray briefly**. Most individuals pray two to four sentences at a time. By each person praying briefly, everyone gets to pray again sooner. This keeps each one alert, awake, and involved in what is being prayed.

4. **Pray spontaneously, not in sequence**. Don't pray around the circle. Let people pray when they are ready and on a topic that interests them. For example, if six subjects are prayed about in the conversational prayer time, you might have a vital interest in only three of them. Praying spontaneously does not mean praying thoughtlessly. While you are listening to another praying on the subject at hand, you have time for the Holy Spirit to confirm in your own heart what you want to pray.

> **CONVERSATIONAL PRAYER GUIDELINES:**
> 1. Don't share—pray.
> 2. One topic at a time.
> 3. Be brief.
> 4. Be spontaneous.

As a group begins conversational prayer, a few moments of silence may be needed for people to quiet their hearts and collect their thoughts. Consider starting with praise and thanksgiving to God and then moving into prayer requests. A common pattern is to pray for needs within the group and then for needs outside the group.

The group leader may need to insert some verbal direction during the prayer time, such as "Would someone pray for the pastor's trip overseas?" or "Let's move on to another topic." The more experience the group has in conversational prayer, the less direction the leader needs to give.

Prayer topics can vary significantly over a period of weeks. During any one of the prayer times, it is really more beneficial to do a thorough job of praying for a few items than to scatter the prayers over too wide a range.

### ASSIGNMENT FOR SESSION 9
1. Scripture Memory: John 5:24 is an optional Scripture memory verse for this course. You have time left to memorize it if you choose. It is an excellent verse to use when explaining your faith in Christ to others. This is a great time to focus on getting all of your memory verses signed off on *My Completion Record*.
2. Quiet Time: Continue reading and marking your Bible and making entries on *My Reading Highlights.*
3. Bible Study: Complete the Bible study "Obedience" (pages 87–91).
4. Other: Complete a list of five to ten non-Christians on an index card and bring it with you for the next session.

# SESSION 9

**OUTLINE OF THIS SESSION**
1. Open the session in prayer.
2. Break into groups of two or three and review all five *Beginning with Christ* verses.
3. Share some highlights from your reading, particularly those you have recorded on *My Reading Highlights*.
4. Discuss the Bible study "Obedience" (pages 87–91).
5. Discuss your evangelism prayer list (page 82).
6. Read "Assignment for Session 10" (page 91).
7. Have a brief time of conversational prayer on two or three topics.

# OBEDIENCE

At the moment we placed our faith in Jesus Christ as Savior and Lord, He called us to a life of obedience. The Holy Spirit set us free from sin and death (Romans 8:2) and came to live within us. The Holy Spirit enables us to live consistently—living Christ's values in a lifestyle that emulates God's biblical teachings.

> It is thus through His atoning death that the penalty of our sins may be forgiven; whereas it is through His indwelling Spirit that the power of our sins may be broken.
>
> —JOHN STOTT

## THINK ABOUT:

What are some similarities between the way children obey their parents and the way Christians obey God? _____

_____

_____

## THE FOUNDATIONS OF OBEDIENCE

When we consider obedience to God, we need to reflect on the wonderfulness of who He is. We are His children, but what kind of children does He want us to be? The Bible is God's blueprint and handbook for us. To obey God's Word is to obey God Himself.

> In John 15, the secret of abounding is abiding, the secret of abiding is obeying, and the secret of obeying is abandonment to Christ.
>
> —WILLIAM A. MIEROP

1. After reflecting on John 14, verses 15 and 21, briefly state the relationship between loving God and obeying Him. _____

_____

_____

2. What were God's instructions for Israel regarding obedience (Deuteronomy 10:12-13)? _____

_____

_____

_____

In what ways might obedience to God be profitable and "for your own good" (verse 13)? _____

_____

_____

_____

> The key to usefulness, to revelation, and to a Holy-Spirit–filled life is obedience to the Word of God.
>
> —DR. JOHN G. "JACK" MITCHELL

## THE PRACTICE OF OBEDIENT LIVING

The obedient Christian still faces daily struggles with temptation and sin. How can you practice obedience and gain victory over sin? Important areas to consider are temptation, sin, confession, and victory.

3. Discover the source and causes of temptation in the following verses:

a. Who is the tempter (Matthew 4:1-3)? _____

b. Who is never the source of temptation (James 1:13)? _____

c. What causes you to be drawn into temptation (James 1:14)? _____

_____

_____

_____

(Lust is desire, especially for what is forbidden.)

4. Using Isaiah 53:6, James 4:17, and 1 John 3:4 as a guide, write a brief

definition of sin. _____

_____

_____

_____

How does sin differ from temptation? _____

_____

_____

_____

While God offers victory and deliverance, men and women can sin because they neglect God's provision. Sins committed but unconfessed hurt God deeply. Although sin does not alter God's love, it does cause a break in fellowship with Him.

5. In Psalm 32:5, David prays and confesses his sin. Please write this verse

in your own words. _____

_____

_____

_____

The practice of continuing to walk close to God can be pictured as follows:

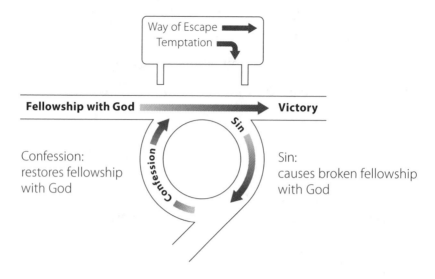

6. Read Romans 6:11-14.

   a. What should we do (verses 11 and 13)? _____

   _____

   b. What should we not do (verses 12 and 13)? _____

   _____

   _____

   _____

   c. What has God promised (verse 14)? _____

   _____

7. Identify and explain what two steps will help you live a life of obedience

   (James 4:7). _____

   _____

   _____

   _____

> Live by the Spirit, and you will not gratify the desires of the
> sinful nature.
>
> —GALATIANS 5:16

## SUMMARY

We show our love to God by obeying the teachings in the Bible and practicing a moral, upright lifestyle. But our diligence in pursuing that kind of life is often challenged by spiritual warfare. To the extent that we appropriate God's provisions for victory, we can live a lifestyle of obedience. We are not immune to temptation, but we don't have to be its victim. Sins do not negate God's love or our salvation, but they do break our fellowship with Him. Sincerely confessing sin restores our fellowship with Him.

## ASSIGNMENT FOR SESSION 10

1. Scripture Memory: Continue to review your *Beginning with Christ* verses every day. Continue memorizing John 5:24 if you are working on that.
2. Quiet Time: You want to continue reading and marking your Bible and making entries on *My Reading Highlights*.
3. Bible Study: Complete the Bible study "Fellowship" (pages 93–98).
4. Other: Finish up any assignments that you can have signed off on *My Completion Record*.

# SESSION 10

1. Open the session in prayer.
2. Break into groups of two or three and quote all your learned memory verses.
3. Share some highlights from your reading, particularly those you have recorded on *My Reading Highlights.*
4. Discuss the Bible study "Fellowship" (pages 93–98).
5. Read "Assignment for Session 11" (page 98).
6. Have a brief time of conversational prayer.

## FELLOWSHIP

> The Church . . . is the body of Christ. Every Christian is a member or organ of the body, while Christ Himself is the Head, controlling the body's activities. Not every organ has the same function, but each is necessary for the maximum health and usefulness of the body. Moreover, the whole body is animated by a common life. This is the Holy Spirit. It is His presence which makes the body one.
>
> —JOHN R. W. STOTT

**THINK ABOUT:**

Picture this situation: Five Christians chat over a cup of coffee. They discuss a recent sports event; the topic moves to "latest high-tech innovations"; someone relates a funny incident that happened to her. Everyone laughs and they begin to talk about the weather forecast for the weekend. As one of them leaves, he says, "I sure do enjoy this good Christian fellowship!"

Is this genuine Christian fellowship? Why or why not? _____

_____

_____

How could their "fellowship" have been improved? _____

_____

_____

### WHAT CONSTITUTES BIBLICAL FELLOWSHIP?

1. God uses the analogy of a body to describe the relationship of believers with one another and with Christ. Who is the Head of the body and why?

   Colossians 1:18 _____

   _____

   _____

2. *Fellowship* is derived from the Greek word *koinonia*, which means "sharing in common." God has given you much to share. As you examine the following verses, determine what you might share with others. In addition, give one practical way it could be shared.

   | | WHAT TO SHARE | A WAY TO SHARE |
   |---|---|---|
   | 1 John 4:11,21 | | |
   | Galatians 6:2 | | |
   | 2 Corinthians 8:13-15 | | |
   | 1 Thessalonians 2:8 | | |
   | James 5:16 | | |

   Sharing involves giving and receiving. Both are integral parts of meaningful fellowship.

3. We Christians fellowship together based on the fact that our sins are forgiven and that we serve the same Lord. The forgiveness we have experienced should affect how we respond to others when we have conflict or have been offended by someone.

   a. What do we learn about broken fellowship from Matthew 5:23-24 and 18:15,35? _____

   _____

   _____

b. Why should reconciliation take priority over worship (Matthew 5:23-24)? _____

_____

_____

We Christians can honestly share our lives. We don't have to pretend to be something we are not.

> The church is the only fellowship in the world where the one requirement for membership is the unworthiness of the candidate.
>
> —ROBERT B. MUNGER

4. Using the following passages, identify some benefits of fellowship.

Proverbs 27:17 _____

Ecclesiastes 4:9-10 _____

Hebrews 3:13 _____
Which benefit could you best help provide for another Christian?

_____

_____

Which of those benefits do you usually receive from other Christians?

_____

_____

**FELLOWSHIP IN THE BODY OF CHRIST**

5. Each believer is given different but important responsibilities in this spiritual body, the Church. Read 1 Corinthians 12:14-27.

a. Who gave the members their various functions (verse 18)? _____

_____

b. What is His desire (verse 25)? _____

_____

c. What attitudes can lead to disharmony in the body (verses 15, 16, and 21)?

_____

_____

_____

d. Why are there no unnecessary functions (members) in the body (verses 20-22)? _____

_____

6. Think of what happens when you hit your finger with a hammer. How does that affect the entire body? _____

_____

_____

How does this illustration parallel the spiritual body (1 Corinthians 12:26)? _____

_____

_____

7. The body works together as one unit, yet it has many specialized organs that perform diverse functions. Summarize in a couple of sentences how both unity and diversity can exist together in the body. _____

_____

_____

8. Examine your attitudes toward other Christians. Is there someone you find difficult to relate to as another member of Christ's body?

a. Why? _____

_____

b. What steps can you take to bring harmony to your relationship with this individual? _____

_____

_____

How wonderful, how beautiful, when brothers and sisters get along!

—Psalm 133:1 (msg)

## THE CHURCH, MANIFESTED LOCALLY

9. What activities of the local church in Jerusalem are mentioned in Acts 2:41-42? _____

_____

_____

_____

### Three distinguishing marks of the early church were
### (1) GENEROSITY (2) PRAYER (3) POWER

10. Read Ephesians 4:11-13. What is the responsibility of apostles, prophets, evangelists, pastors, and teachers? _____

_____

_____

What should be the end result of this process (Ephesians 4:13)? _____

_____

11. What are some responsibilities we have to one another in a fellowship of believers?

Ephesians 5:21 _____

Colossians 3:16 _____

1 Thessalonians 5:11 _____

Hebrews 10:24-25 _____

James 5:16 _____

In which of these responsibilities do you think you could best contribute to meeting needs among other believers? Explain briefly. _____

_____

_____

_____

12. Review your answers in this Bible study. List two reasons why you believe that fellowship is indispensable. _____

_____

_____

_____

_____

We, numerous as we are, are one body in Christ (the
Messiah) and individually we are parts one of another
[mutually dependent on one another].

—ROMANS 12:5 (AMP)

## SUMMARY

Genuine fellowship is based on the concept of giving and receiving among
Christians. We can contribute possessions, musical talent, compassionate listening, a verse of Scripture—many things God has given us to share. God
promotes fellowship for the purpose of our mutual encouragement and growth.
He delights when Christians live together in unity and harmony.

In the Bible, God explains the working relationship among believers, using
the analogy of the body. Jesus Christ is the Head of the body. All Christians
throughout the world belong to Christ's body, but God wants us to relate to a
smaller, specific group of believers—in a local church. This smaller group is
for the purpose of instruction, sharing, worship, and service. God has given
spiritual leaders to model evangelism and to help believers mature in Christ
and become effective in ministry.

## ASSIGNMENT FOR SESSION 11

1. Scripture Memory: Study "Why Memorize Scripture" (pages 99–100):
   a. Part 1—List at least five reasons why a person would want to memorize Scripture.
   b. Part 2—List one or two reasons why you memorize Scripture.
2. Quiet Time: Continue reading and marking your Bible and making
   entries on *My Reading Highlights*.
3. Bible Study: Complete the Bible study "Witness" (pages 100–104).

# SESSION 11

1. Open the session in prayer.
2. Break into groups of two or three and review your five or six memory verses; work on getting items initialed on *My Completion Record*.
3. Share at least one item from *My Reading Highlights* with your group.
4. Check to see that all items on *My Completion Record* are initialed and that your leader has signed the entry "Graduated from *Growing Strong in God's Family.*"
5. Discuss "Why Memorize Scripture" (pages 99–100).
6. Discuss the Bible study "Witness" (pages 100–104).
7. Read aloud "Keep Growing" (pages 104–105).
8. Have a brief time of conversational prayer.

## WHY MEMORIZE SCRIPTURE

### PART 1
List some of the reasons why a person would memorize Scripture.

_____

_____

_____

_____

**PART 2**

  a.  The primary personal benefit I expect from Scripture memory is (if you wish, list other benefits that strongly motivate you to continue memorizing Scripture): _____

_____

_____

_____

_____

  b.  One or two attitudes or influences that could hinder my success in meaningful Scripture memory are: _____

_____

_____

_____

_____

_____

## WITNESS

It is the Holy Spirit, not we, who converts an individual. We, the privileged ambassadors of Jesus Christ, can communicate a verbal message; we can demonstrate through our personality and life what the grace of Jesus Christ can accomplish. . . . But let us never naively think that we have converted a soul and brought him to Jesus Christ. . . . No one calls Jesus Lord except by the Holy Spirit.

—Paul Little

## THE CHALLENGE

1. What is the cause-and-effect relationship in Jesus' statement found in Matthew 4:19? _____

   _____

   _____

   _____

   _____

2. In Mark 5:19, you'll discover Jesus' desire concerning a man He has healed.

   a. Where did He send him? _____

   b. What did He tell him to do? _____

   c. Why do you suppose Jesus gave these particular instructions?

   _____

   _____

   _____

   d. What application can we draw from this account? _____

   _____

   _____

   _____

   _____

3. Carefully examine 2 Corinthians 5:9-14. In this section, Paul lists several motivations and reasons for witnessing for Christ.

   a. List those you discover.

   Verse 9 _____

   Verse 10 _____

Verse 11 _____

Verse 14 _____

b. Read verse 20. Using resources such as dictionaries and encyclopedias, briefly define or describe "an ambassador's function." _____

_____

_____

_____

_____

_____


## PRESENTING THE MESSAGE

4. What is the gospel as stated in 1 Corinthians 15:1-4? _____

_____

_____

_____

_____

5. Read 1 Corinthians 15:12-19 and list several reasons why the Resurrection is an essential part of the gospel message. _____

_____

_____

_____

_____

6. What attitudes did Paul have about sharing the gospel?

Acts 20:24 _____

_____

Romans 1:15-16 _____

_____

Mark an "X" on the line to indicate where you feel you are now in your attitude about sharing the gospel.

•————————————————————————————————————————————•

Ashamed of the gospel                                    Eager to preach the gospel

## THE MESSENGER

> God hasn't engaged many of us to be lawyers, but He has
> summoned all of us as witnesses.
>
> —UNKNOWN

Witnessing is not merely an activity; it is a way of life. Christians don't do witnessing; they are witnesses, good or bad. We want to keep improving our witness for Jesus Christ.

7. In your own words, rewrite Romans 10:13-15. _____

_____

_____

_____

_____

Some people never read the Bible and seldom attend church, but when they hear what Christ has done for you, they are often open to hearing what Christ can do for them.

8. Peter wrote encouraging instructions regarding witnessing to Christians who were enduring significant suffering. The guidelines still apply today.

   a. In 1 Peter 3:15-16, what does Peter suggest regarding witnessing?

   _____

   _____

   _____

   b. Which of Peter's suggestions do you think is the most important and why?

   _____

   _____

   _____

9. What are some steps you could take to become a more effective witness?

   _____

   _____

You are writing a gospel, a chapter each day,
    By the deeds that you do and the words that you say.
People read what you write—distorted or true;
    What is the gospel according to you?

—LEROY BROWNLOW

## SUMMARY

God has summoned each Christian to be a witness of what he or she has "seen and heard" (1 John 1:3). Witnessing is part of a lifestyle; people observe the way we live our lives. Actions often speak louder than words. Yet our actions are not sufficient for communicating to another person the message of the gospel of Christ. We also need to witness by our words—to identify openly with Jesus Christ and clearly communicate the message of how a person can be reconciled to God. We can effectively communicate the gospel by telling our salvation story and sharing examples of how God continues to work in our lives.

# KEEP GROWING

### WHAT YOU HAVE ACCOMPLISHED

During *Growing Strong in God's Family,* you have taken significant steps toward firmly establishing your walk with Christ. Your Christian life has been built up by:

- Learning to enjoy Bible reading and marking
- Experiencing a consistent and meaningful quiet time with the Lord, and recording daily quiet time thoughts
- Memorizing five or six key Scripture passages for developing your walk with Christ, and deepening your convictions about the importance of memorizing Scripture
- Discovering Bible principles for maintaining a balanced Christian life
- Developing an evangelism prayer list and considering ways to develop friendships with non-Christians

**Congratulations on your diligence in completing *Growing Strong in God's Family*!**

THE 2:7 SERIES

> Rooted and built up in him, strengthened in the faith as you
> were taught, and overflowing with thankfulness.
> —COLOSSIANS 2:7

As you know, there are three excellent courses in THE 2:7 SERIES. Book 2 builds
on the work completed in book 1. Book 3 builds on what was accomplished in
book 2. Plan to complete all three courses.

## A PREVIEW OF BOOK 2

Now that you have completed book 1, you can look forward to the next excellent training segment: *Deepening Your Roots in God's Family.*

- Book 1: *Growing Strong in God's Family*
- Book 2: *Deepening Your Roots in God's Family*
- Book 3: *Bearing Fruit in God's Family*

In book 2, you will continue to develop your walk with Christ by:

- Memorizing verses on the six parts of The Wheel Illustration
- Learning how to prepare and present "My Story," a brief, clear
  explanation of how you received God's salvation
- Learning how to spend an extended time alone with God
- Reading and discussing an interesting analogy of how the lordship of
  Christ can work in our lives
- Studying scriptural principles for walking with Christ

Studying book 2 will be very much worth the investment of your time and
effort. You will experience the benefits for years to come!

# APPENDIX

- All the memory verses from book 1—printed out so you can choose a translation for your memory work (pages 109–113)
- The Bridge Illustration (pages 115–121)
- My Reading Highlights—copies you can use (pages 123–152)
- My Reading Progress—one copy for this course (pages 153–154)

# BOOK 1 MEMORY VERSES

From the following pages, please select the translation you prefer for your memory work in book 1.

## *New International Version (NIV-1984)*

### ASSURANCE OF SALVATION

1 John 5:11-12
And this is the testimony: God has given us eternal life, and this life is in his Son. He who has the Son has life; he who does not have the Son of God does not have life.

1 John 5:11-12

### ASSURANCE OF FORGIVENESS

1 John 1:9
If we confess our sins, he is faithful and just and will forgive us our sins and purify us from all unrighteousness.

1 John 1:9

### ASSURANCE OF ANSWERED PRAYER

John 16:24
Until now you have not asked for anything in my name. Ask and you will receive, and your joy will be complete.

John 16:24

### ASSURANCE OF GUIDANCE

Proverbs 3:5-6
Trust in the Lord with all your heart and lean not on your own understanding; in all your ways acknowledge him, and he will make your paths straight.

Proverbs 3:5-6

### ASSURANCE OF VICTORY

1 Corinthians 10:13
No temptation has seized you except what is common to man. And God is faithful; he will not let you be tempted beyond what you can bear. But when you are tempted, he will also provide a way out so that you can stand up under it.

1 Corinthians 10:13

### OPTIONAL OUTREACH VERSE

John 5:24
I tell you the truth, whoever hears my word and believes him who sent me has eternal life and will not be condemned; he has crossed over from death to life.

John 5:24

# New American Standard Bible (NASB)

## ASSURANCE OF SALVATION

1 John 5:11-12

And the testimony is this, that God has given us eternal life, and this life is in His Son. He who has the Son has the life; he who does not have the Son of God does not have the life.

1 John 5:11-12

## ASSURANCE OF ANSWERED PRAYER

John 16:24

Until now you have asked for nothing in My name; ask and you will receive, so that your joy may be made full.

John 16:24

## ASSURANCE OF VICTORY

1 Corinthians 10:13

No temptation has overtaken you but such as is common to man; and God is faithful, who will not allow you to be tempted beyond what you are able, but with the temptation will provide the way of escape also, so that you will be able to endure it.

1 Corinthians 10:13

## ASSURANCE OF FORGIVENESS

1 John 1:9

If we confess our sins, He is faithful and righteous to forgive us our sins and to cleanse us from all unrighteousness.

1 John 1:9

## ASSURANCE OF GUIDANCE

Proverbs 3:5-6

Trust in the LORD with all your heart and do not lean on your own understanding. In all your ways acknowledge Him, and He will make your paths straight.

Proverbs 3:5-6

## OPTIONAL OUTREACH VERSE

John 5:24

Truly, truly, I say to you, he who hears My word, and believes Him who sent Me, has eternal life, and does not come into judgment, but has passed out of death into life.

John 5:24

## ASSURANCE OF SALVATION

1 John 5:11-12

And this is the record, that God hath given to us eternal life, and this life is in his Son. He that hath the Son hath life; and he that hath not the Son of God hath not life.

1 John 5:11-12

## ASSURANCE OF ANSWERED PRAYER

John 16:24

Hitherto have ye asked nothing in my name: ask, and ye shall receive, that your joy may be full.

John 16:24

## ASSURANCE OF VICTORY

1 Corinthians 10:13

There hath no temptation taken you but such as is common to man: but God is faithful, who will not suffer you to be tempted above that ye are able; but will with the temptation also make a way to escape, that ye may be able to bear it.

1 Corinthians 10:13

## ASSURANCE OF FORGIVENESS

1 John 1:9

If we confess our sins, he is faithful and just to forgive us our sins, and to cleanse us from all unrighteousness.

1 John 1:9

## ASSURANCE OF GUIDANCE

Proverbs 3:5-6

Trust in the Lord with all thine heart; and lean not unto thine own understanding. In all thy ways acknowledge him, and he shall direct thy paths.

Proverbs 3:5-6

## OPTIONAL OUTREACH VERSE

John 5:24

Verily, verily, I say unto you, He that heareth my word, and believeth on him that sent me, hath everlasting life, and shall not come into condemnation; but is passed from death unto life.

John 5:24

# *New King James Version (NKJV)*

## ASSURANCE OF SALVATION

1 John 5:11-12

And this is the testimony: that God has given us eternal life, and this life is in His Son. He who has the Son has life; he who does not have the Son of God does not have life.

1 John 5:11-12

## ASSURANCE OF ANSWERED PRAYER

John 16:24

Until now you have asked nothing in My name. Ask, and you will receive, that your joy may be full.

John 16:24

## ASSURANCE OF VICTORY

1 Corinthians 10:13

No temptation has overtaken you except such as is common to man; but God is faithful, who will not allow you to be tempted beyond what you are able, but with the temptation will also make the way of escape, that you may be able to bear it.

1 Corinthians 10:13

## ASSURANCE OF FORGIVENESS

1 John 1:9

If we confess our sins, He is faithful and just to forgive us our sins and to cleanse us from all unrighteousness.

1 John 1:9

## ASSURANCE OF GUIDANCE

Proverbs 3:5-6

Trust in the Lᴏʀᴅ with all your heart, and lean not on your own understanding; in all your ways acknowledge Him, and He shall direct your paths.

Proverbs 3:5-6

## OPTIONAL OUTREACH VERSE

John 5:24

Most assuredly, I say to you, he who hears My word and believes in Him who sent Me has everlasting life, and shall not come into judgment, but has passed from death into life.

John 5:24

# New Revised Standard Version (NRSV)

## ASSURANCE OF SALVATION

1 John 5:11-12

And this is the testimony: God gave us eternal life, and this life is in his Son. Whoever has the Son has life; whoever does not have the Son of God does not have life.

1 John 5:11-12

## ASSURANCE OF ANSWERED PRAYER

John 16:24

Until now you have not asked for anything in my name. Ask and you will receive, so that your joy may be complete.

John 16:24

## ASSURANCE OF VICTORY

1 Corinthians 10:13

No testing has overtaken you that is not common to everyone. God is faithful, and he will not let you be tested beyond your strength, but with the testing he will also provide the way out so that you may be able to endure it.

1 Corinthians 10:13

## ASSURANCE OF FORGIVENESS

1 John 1:9

If we confess our sins, he who is faithful and just will forgive us our sins and cleanse us from all unrighteousness.

1 John 1:9

## ASSURANCE OF GUIDANCE

Proverbs 3:5-6

Trust in the LORD with all your heart, and do not rely on your own insight. In all your ways acknowledge him, and he will make straight your paths.

Proverbs 3:5-6

## OPTIONAL OUTREACH VERSE

John 5:24

Very truly, I tell you, anyone who hears my word and believes him who sent me has eternal life, and does not come under judgment, but has passed from death to life.

John 5:24

# THE BRIDGE ILLUSTRATION

## *A Summary of the Gospel of Jesus Christ*

History and archeology document Jesus Christ, the apostle Paul, and others as having actually lived in the places and situations described in the Bible. We can trust the Bible! The Bible shows us who God is, reveals His plans and purposes, and explains to us how to allow God to renovate our lives in ways that please Him and benefit us.

The Bible teaches that we all tend to stray onto paths contrary to God's plans and purposes for us and for the world. Often people are unaware of their need for reconciliation with God. We can too easily neglect Him and follow our own independent paths.

The Bridge Illustration explains from the Bible how a person can become a true follower of Christ and receive the gift of eternal life. It has been used in many languages, cultures, and across a broad spectrum of denominations and religious backgrounds. To you, it may be a review of what you already have applied to your life. Or some of these Bible truths may be brand-new. "Examine yourselves to see whether you are in the faith" (2 Corinthians 13:5).

As you read each Bible verse, you will find it helpful to locate where it is used on the graphic. For example, Romans 6:23 (the book of Romans, chapter 6 and verse 23) is part of describing "Our Problem." You don't need to look up the verses in a Bible; they are supplied for you in the text.

## 1. GOD'S PURPOSE

&lt; John 10:10   Full, Abundant Life
   John 3:16   Eternal Life

**God loves us and offers us a full, abundant life, and eternal life.**

In John 10:10, Jesus said, "I have come that they may have life, and have it to the full."

US

GOD

For God so loved the world that he gave his one and only Son, that whoever believes in him shall not perish but have eternal life. —JOHN 3:16

Why are so many people not experiencing this kind of life? We see part of the answer in the Bible's description of the BAD NEWS side of our situation. Later we look at the good news side.

## 2. OUR PROBLEM

The Ten Commandments and other Bible passages define God's guidelines for human behavior—which are impossible to follow and obey perfectly. And God did not create us as robots to automatically love and obey Him—He gave us a will and freedom of choice.

**None of us has met God's standards of morality.** In many ways and to varying degrees we all have sinned and continue to sin. **Our sins seperate us from God.**

For all have sinned and fall short of the glory of God.  —ROMANS 3:23

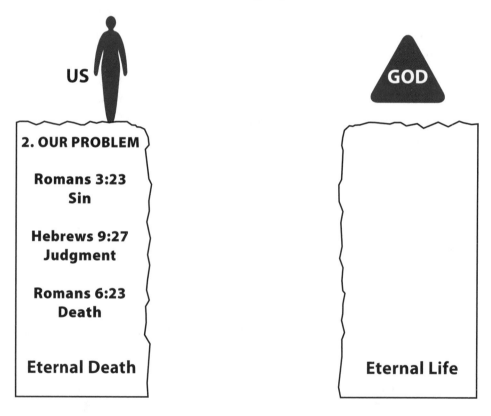

Each of us will die physically and then stand before God as our judge.

Just as man is destined to die once, and after that to face judgment.
—HEBREWS 9:27

God will judge us and then reluctantly assign us to the consequence of our sins—eternal death and separation from God.

For the wages of sin is death, but the gift of God is eternal life in Christ Jesus our Lord. —Romans 6:23

Understanding our terrible dilemma should compel us to repent, which is having "godly sorrow for one's sin and a resolve to turn from it."⁴ We must turn from sin toward God.

The Lord is not slow in keeping his promise. . . . He is patient with you, not wanting anyone to perish, but everyone to come to repentance. —2 Peter 3:9

**God wants a close relationship with us and has provided the remedy for our alienation from Him. Here is the GOOD NEWS of the gospel.**

## 3. GOD'S REMEDY

**Jesus Christ died on the cross and rose from the dead, paying the penalty for our sins and bridging the gap between us and God.**

But God demonstrates his own love for us in this: While we were still sinners, Christ died for us. —Romans 5:8

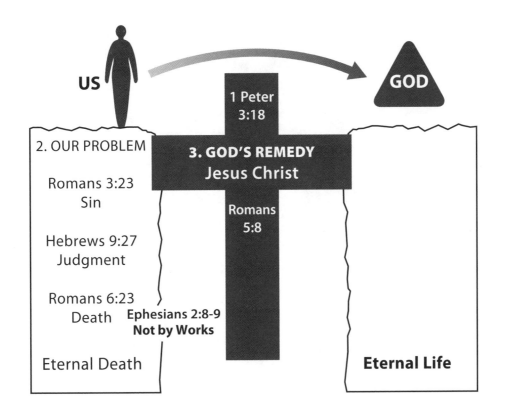

For Christ died for sins once for all, the righteous for the unrighteous, to bring you to God. —1 Peter 3:18

It is incredible, but Christ died in our place. He took the penalty for our sins on Himself on the cross.

**A common misconception**: Some people believe that God is keeping score of what they do, whether right or wrong, and that at their death God compares the scores. They assume that if they have done more good than bad, they go to heaven. But the Bible is clear—eternal life is a free gift that cannot be earned by good works or deeds. Our good works do not bridge the gap.

For it is by grace you have been saved, through faith—and this not from yourselves, it is the gift of God—not by works, so that no one can boast. —Ephesians 2:8-9

Please also see Romans 6:23 under "Our Problem."

**Only by appropriating Christ's death on the cross can a person have the certainty of eternal life**.

## 4. OUR RESPONSE

God sees inside our hearts and minds. In a prayer to God, express your gratitude for Christ's death on the cross for you, and **by personal invitation** ask Christ to be your own Savior and Lord.

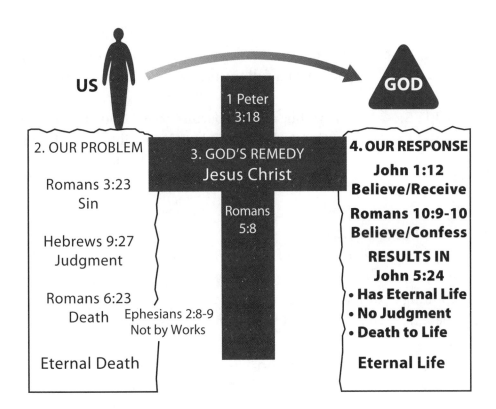

1. GOD'S PURPOSE
John 10:10   Full, Abundant Life
John 3:16   Eternal Life

US     GOD

1 Peter 3:18

2. OUR PROBLEM

Romans 3:23
Sin

Hebrews 9:27
Judgment

Romans 6:23
Death   Ephesians 2:8-9
Not by Works

Eternal Death

3. GOD'S REMEDY
Jesus Christ

Romans 5:8

4. OUR RESPONSE

John 1:12
Believe/Receive

Romans 10:9-10
Believe/Confess

RESULTS IN
John 5:24
• Has Eternal Life
• No Judgment
• Death to Life

Eternal Life

Yet to all who received him, to those who believed in his name, he gave the right to become children of God. —John 1:12

That if you confess with your mouth, "Jesus is Lord," and believe in your heart that God raised him from the dead, you will be saved. For it is with your heart that you believe and are justified, and it is with your mouth that you confess and are saved. —Romans 10:9-10

Christ's resurrection proves His Deity and validates His promise that believers' sins are forgiven. He lives again—so shall believers!

**Next, let's look at John 5:24 and a summary of how we can make our response to the Gospel of Jesus Christ.**

### HEARING, BELIEVING, RECEIVING

I tell you the truth, whoever *hears* my word and *believes* him who sent me has eternal life and will not be condemned; he has crossed over from death to life. —JOHN 5:24, EMPHASIS ADDED

**HEAR:** Do you understand the Bible message in The Bridge Illustration? Have you really heard it?

**BELIEVE:** In your heart do you understand and believe that Christ died on the cross for you and rose from the dead—that you are putting your full trust in Christ's death on your behalf?

**RECEIVE:** Are you willing to reach out and accept God's gift of eternal life—realizing that when Christ comes into your life in this way, He may begin to renovate your life in ways that could be uncomfortable, but best for you?

### HOW TO RECEIVE CHRIST

1. Admit your need. (I have sinned and done many things wrong, which God will judge.)
2. Be willing to turn from your sins. (Repent.)
3. Believe that Jesus Christ died for you on the cross and rose from the dead.
4. Through prayer, invite Jesus Christ to come in and control your life through the Holy Spirit. (Receive Him as Lord and Savior of your life.)

### PRAYER OF COMMITMENT

(If you are alone, pray aloud). You might thoughtfully and sincerely talk to God in a prayer something like this:

Heavenly Father, I thank you that you love me deeply just the way I am—that you care about me and want the very best for me.

I understand and believe that I have done many things wrong in your sight. I have sinned in various ways, and I know that those things have hurt you deeply.

I also understand and believe that the penalty for my sins is eternal death—that I cannot be with you in heaven without having all of my sins forgiven.

I thank you so much that you sent your Son Jesus Christ to die on the cross for me—the sacrifice that paid for all of my sins. Thank you, Jesus Christ, for dying in my place—willingly enduring the horrible beatings and crucifixion that give me forgiveness and make me righteous in the eyes of God the Father.

Right now, Jesus Christ, I ask you to come into my heart and life. Please apply your death on the cross to me personally. I am willing for you to take over my life and to lead me on the best path. I give you permission to work in my life—to help me change and grow and become all that you want me to be.

I pray these things sincerely from my heart. Thank you for hearing me! I pray in the name of Jesus Christ, your Son. Amen.

**WHERE DO I GO FROM HERE?**

1. Share with a like-minded Christian that you have made this commitment to Christ.
2. Join a group that can help you grow in your Christian life. Sometimes one mature Christian can become a mentor for you.
   a. Learn practical ways to read and study your Bible (to know God better and to find helpful things to apply to your life).
   b. Learn more about talking to God in prayer (to pray for yourself and for others).
   c. Learn effective ways to explain your faith in Christ to others.
   d. Learn more about what God has done through history and what He is doing now.
3. Be part of a church where Christ is preached and the Bible is taught.
4. Develop a band of Christian friends you spend time with—to offset negative influences and together to help others come to faith in Christ.

# MY READING HIGHLIGHTS

"Now, my children, listen to me. Those who follow my ways are happy. Listen to my teaching, and you will be wise. Do not ignore it. Those who listen to me are happy. They stand watching at my door every day. They are at my open door waiting to be with me." —Proverbs 8:32-34 (NCV)

Translation _____ Year _____

☐ **Sunday** Date _____ All I read today _____

Best thing I marked today: *Reference* _____

*Thought:* _____

_____

How it impressed me: _____

_____

_____

_____

☐ **Monday** Date _____ All I read today _____

Best thing I marked today: *Reference* _____

*Thought:* _____

_____

How it impressed me: _____

_____

_____

_____

☐ **Tuesday** Date _____ All I read today _____

Best thing I marked today: *Reference* _____

*Thought:* _____

_____

How it impressed me: _____

_____

_____

_____

**124**

APPENDIX

☐ **Wednesday** Date _____ All I read today _____

Best thing I marked today: *Reference* _____

*Thought:* _____

_____

How it impressed me: _____

_____

_____


☐ **Thursday** Date _____ All I read today _____

Best thing I marked today: *Reference* _____

*Thought:* _____

_____

How it impressed me: _____

_____

_____

_____


☐ **Friday** Date _____ All I read today _____

Best thing I marked today: *Reference* _____

*Thought:* _____

_____

How it impressed me: _____

_____

_____

_____


☐ **Saturday** Date _____ All I read today _____

Best thing I marked today: *Reference* _____

*Thought:* _____

_____

How it impressed me: _____

_____

_____

_____

# MY READING HIGHLIGHTS

"Now, my children, listen to me. Those who follow my ways are happy. Listen to my teaching, and you will be wise.  Do not ignore it. Those who listen to me are happy. They stand watching at my door every day. They are at my open door waiting to be with me." —Proverbs 8:32-34 (NCV)

Translation _____ Year _____

☐ **Sunday** Date _____ All I read today _____

Best thing I marked today: *Reference* _____

*Thought:* _____

_____

How it impressed me: _____

_____

_____

☐ **Monday** Date _____ All I read today _____

Best thing I marked today: *Reference* _____

*Thought:* _____

_____

How it impressed me: _____

_____

_____

_____

☐ **Tuesday** Date _____ All I read today _____

Best thing I marked today: *Reference* _____

*Thought:* _____

_____

How it impressed me: _____

_____

_____

☐ **Wednesday** Date _____ All I read today _____

Best thing I marked today: *Reference* _____

*Thought:* _____

_____

How it impressed me: _____

_____

_____

_____


☐ **Thursday** Date _____ All I read today _____

Best thing I marked today: *Reference* _____

*Thought:* _____

_____

How it impressed me: _____

_____

_____

_____


☐ **Friday** Date _____ All I read today _____

Best thing I marked today: *Reference* _____

*Thought:* _____

_____

How it impressed me: _____

_____

_____

_____


☐ **Saturday** Date _____ All I read today _____

Best thing I marked today: *Reference* _____

*Thought:* _____

_____

How it impressed me: _____

_____

_____

_____

# MY READING HIGHLIGHTS

"Now, my children, listen to me. Those who follow my ways are happy. Listen to my teaching, and you will be wise. Do not ignore it. Those who listen to me are happy. They stand watching at my door every day. They are at my open door waiting to be with me." —Proverbs 8:32-34 (NCV)

Translation _____ Year _____

☐ **Sunday** Date _____ All I read today _____

Best thing I marked today: *Reference* _____

*Thought:* _____

_____

How it impressed me: _____

_____

_____

_____

☐ **Monday** Date _____ All I read today _____

Best thing I marked today: *Reference* _____

*Thought:* _____

_____

How it impressed me: _____

_____

_____

_____

☐ **Tuesday** Date _____ All I read today _____

Best thing I marked today: *Reference* _____

*Thought:* _____

_____

How it impressed me: _____

_____

_____

_____

☐ **Wednesday** Date_____ All I read today _____

Best thing I marked today: *Reference* _____

*Thought:* _____

_____

How it impressed me: _____

_____

_____

_____

☐ **Thursday** Date_____ All I read today _____

Best thing I marked today: *Reference* _____

*Thought:* _____

_____

How it impressed me: _____

_____

_____

_____

_____

☐ **Friday** Date_____ All I read today _____

Best thing I marked today: *Reference* _____

*Thought:* _____

_____

How it impressed me: _____

_____

_____

_____

☐ **Saturday** Date_____ All I read today _____

Best thing I marked today: *Reference* _____

*Thought:* _____

_____

How it impressed me: _____

_____

_____

_____

# MY READING HIGHLIGHTS

"Now, my children, listen to me. Those who follow my ways are happy. Listen to my teaching, and you will be wise. Do not ignore it. Those who listen to me are happy. They stand watching at my door every day. They are at my open door waiting to be with me." —Proverbs 8:32-34 (NCV)

Translation _____ Year _____

☐ **Sunday** Date _____ All I read today _____

Best thing I marked today: *Reference* _____

*Thought:* _____

_____

How it impressed me: _____

_____

_____

_____

☐ **Monday** Date _____ All I read today _____

Best thing I marked today: *Reference* _____

*Thought:* _____

_____

How it impressed me: _____

_____

_____

_____

☐ **Tuesday** Date _____ All I read today _____

Best thing I marked today: *Reference* _____

*Thought:* _____

_____

How it impressed me: _____

_____

_____

☐ **Wednesday** Date_____ All I read today _____

Best thing I marked today: *Reference* _____

*Thought:* _____

How it impressed me: _____


☐ **Thursday** Date_____ All I read today _____

Best thing I marked today: *Reference* _____

*Thought:* _____

How it impressed me: _____


☐ **Friday** Date_____ All I read today _____

Best thing I marked today: *Reference* _____

*Thought:* _____

How it impressed me: _____


☐ **Saturday** Date_____ All I read today _____

Best thing I marked today: *Reference* _____

*Thought:* _____

How it impressed me: _____

# MY READING HIGHLIGHTS

"Now, my children, listen to me. Those who follow my ways are happy. Listen to my teaching, and you will be wise.  Do not ignore it. Those who listen to me are happy. They stand watching at my door every day. They are at my open door waiting to be with me." —Proverbs 8:32-34 (NCV)

Translation _____ Year _____

☐ **Sunday** Date _____ All I read today _____

Best thing I marked today: *Reference* _____

*Thought:* _____

_____

How it impressed me: _____

_____

_____

_____

☐ **Monday** Date _____ All I read today _____

Best thing I marked today: *Reference* _____

*Thought:* _____

_____

How it impressed me: _____

_____

_____

_____

☐ **Tuesday** Date _____ All I read today _____

Best thing I marked today: *Reference* _____

*Thought:* _____

_____

How it impressed me: _____

_____

_____

☐ **Wednesday** Date _____ All I read today _____

Best thing I marked today: *Reference* _____

*Thought:* _____

_____

How it impressed me: _____

_____

_____

☐ **Thursday** Date _____ All I read today _____

Best thing I marked today: *Reference* _____

*Thought:* _____

_____

How it impressed me: _____

_____

_____

☐ **Friday** Date _____ All I read today _____

Best thing I marked today: *Reference* _____

*Thought:* _____

_____

How it impressed me: _____

_____

_____

☐ **Saturday** Date _____ All I read today _____

Best thing I marked today: *Reference* _____

*Thought:* _____

_____

How it impressed me: _____

_____

_____

## MY READING HIGHLIGHTS

"Now, my children, listen to me. Those who follow my ways are happy. Listen to my teaching, and you will be wise.  Do not ignore it. Those who listen to me are happy. They stand watching at my door every day. They are at my open door waiting to be with me." —Proverbs 8:32-34 (NCV)

Translation _____ Year _____

☐ **Sunday** Date _____ All I read today _____

Best thing I marked today: *Reference* _____

*Thought:* _____

_____

How it impressed me: _____

_____

_____

☐ **Monday** Date _____ All I read today _____

Best thing I marked today: *Reference* _____

*Thought:* _____

_____

How it impressed me: _____

_____

_____

☐ **Tuesday** Date _____ All I read today _____

Best thing I marked today: *Reference* _____

*Thought:* _____

_____

How it impressed me: _____

_____

_____

☐ **Wednesday** Date_____ All I read today _____

Best thing I marked today: *Reference* _____

*Thought:* _____

_____

How it impressed me: _____

_____

_____

_____

☐ **Thursday** Date_____ All I read today _____

Best thing I marked today: *Reference* _____

*Thought:* _____

_____

How it impressed me: _____

_____

_____

_____

☐ **Friday** Date _____ All I read today _____

Best thing I marked today: *Reference* _____

*Thought:* _____

_____

How it impressed me: _____

_____

_____

_____

☐ **Saturday** Date _____ All I read today _____

Best thing I marked today: *Reference* _____

*Thought:* _____

_____

How it impressed me: _____

_____

_____

_____

# MY READING HIGHLIGHTS

"Now, my children, listen to me. Those who follow my ways are happy. Listen to my teaching, and you will be wise. Do not ignore it. Those who listen to me are happy. They stand watching at my door every day. They are at my open door waiting to be with me." —Proverbs 8:32-34 (NCV)

Translation _____ Year _____

☐ **Sunday** Date _____ All I read today _____

Best thing I marked today: *Reference* _____

*Thought:* _____

How it impressed me: _____

☐ **Monday** Date _____ All I read today _____

Best thing I marked today: *Reference* _____

*Thought:* _____

How it impressed me: _____

☐ **Tuesday** Date _____ All I read today _____

Best thing I marked today: *Reference* _____

*Thought:* _____

How it impressed me: _____

☐ **Wednesday** Date _____ All I read today _____

Best thing I marked today: *Reference* _____

*Thought:* _____

How it impressed me: _____

☐ **Thursday** Date _____ All I read today _____

Best thing I marked today: *Reference* _____

*Thought:* _____

How it impressed me: _____

☐ **Friday** Date _____ All I read today _____

Best thing I marked today: *Reference* _____

*Thought:* _____

How it impressed me: _____

☐ **Saturday** Date _____ All I read today _____

Best thing I marked today: *Reference* _____

*Thought:* _____

How it impressed me: _____

# MY READING HIGHLIGHTS

"Now, my children, listen to me. Those who follow my ways are happy. Listen to my teaching, and you will be wise.  Do not ignore it. Those who listen to me are happy. They stand watching at my door every day. They are at my open door waiting to be with me." —Proverbs 8:32-34 (NCV)

Translation _____ Year _____

☐ **Sunday** Date _____ All I read today _____

Best thing I marked today: *Reference* _____

*Thought:* _____

_____

How it impressed me: _____

_____

_____

_____

☐ **Monday** Date _____ All I read today _____

Best thing I marked today: *Reference* _____

*Thought:* _____

_____

How it impressed me: _____

_____

_____

_____

☐ **Tuesday** Date _____ All I read today _____

Best thing I marked today: *Reference* _____

*Thought:* _____

_____

How it impressed me: _____

_____

_____

_____

☐ **Wednesday** Date _____ All I read today _____

Best thing I marked today: *Reference* _____

*Thought:* _____

_____

How it impressed me: _____

_____

_____

_____


☐ **Thursday** Date _____ All I read today _____

Best thing I marked today: *Reference* _____

*Thought:* _____

_____

How it impressed me: _____

_____

_____

_____


☐ **Friday** Date _____ All I read today _____

Best thing I marked today: *Reference* _____

*Thought:* _____

_____

How it impressed me: _____

_____

_____

_____


☐ **Saturday** Date _____ All I read today _____

Best thing I marked today: *Reference* _____

*Thought:* _____

_____

How it impressed me: _____

_____

_____

_____

# MY READING HIGHLIGHTS

"Now, my children, listen to me. Those who follow my ways are happy. Listen to my teaching, and you will be wise. Do not ignore it. Those who listen to me are happy. They stand watching at my door every day. They are at my open door waiting to be with me." —Proverbs 8:32-34 (NCV)

Translation _____ Year _____

☐ **Sunday** Date _____ All I read today _____

Best thing I marked today: *Reference* _____

*Thought:* _____

_____

How it impressed me: _____

_____

_____

_____

☐ **Monday** Date _____ All I read today _____

Best thing I marked today: *Reference* _____

*Thought:* _____

_____

How it impressed me: _____

_____

_____

_____

☐ **Tuesday** Date _____ All I read today _____

Best thing I marked today: *Reference* _____

*Thought:* _____

_____

How it impressed me: _____

_____

_____

_____

☐ **Wednesday** Date_____ All I read today _____

Best thing I marked today: *Reference* _____

*Thought:* _____

_____

How it impressed me: _____

_____

_____

☐ **Thursday** Date_____ All I read today _____

Best thing I marked today: *Reference* _____

*Thought:* _____

_____

How it impressed me: _____

_____

_____

_____

☐ **Friday** Date_____ All I read today _____

Best thing I marked today: *Reference* _____

*Thought:* _____

_____

How it impressed me: _____

_____

_____

_____

☐ **Saturday** Date_____ All I read today _____

Best thing I marked today: *Reference* _____

*Thought:* _____

_____

How it impressed me: _____

_____

_____

_____

# MY READING HIGHLIGHTS

"Now, my children, listen to me. Those who follow my ways are happy. Listen to my teaching, and you will be wise. Do not ignore it. Those who listen to me are happy. They stand watching at my door every day. They are at my open door waiting to be with me." —Proverbs 8:32-34 (NCV)

Translation _____ Year _____

☐ **Sunday** Date _____ All I read today _____

Best thing I marked today: *Reference* _____

*Thought:* _____

_____

How it impressed me: _____

_____

_____

☐ **Monday** Date _____ All I read today _____

Best thing I marked today: *Reference* _____

*Thought:* _____

_____

How it impressed me: _____

_____

_____

_____

☐ **Tuesday** Date _____ All I read today _____

Best thing I marked today: *Reference* _____

*Thought:* _____

_____

How it impressed me: _____

_____

_____

☐ **Wednesday** Date_____ All I read today _____

Best thing I marked today: *Reference* _____

*Thought:* _____

_____

How it impressed me: _____

_____

_____

_____

☐ **Thursday** Date _____ All I read today _____

Best thing I marked today: *Reference* _____

*Thought:* _____

_____

How it impressed me: _____

_____

_____

_____

☐ **Friday** Date _____ All I read today _____

Best thing I marked today: *Reference* _____

*Thought:* _____

_____

How it impressed me: _____

_____

_____

_____

☐ **Saturday** Date _____ All I read today _____

Best thing I marked today: *Reference* _____

*Thought:* _____

_____

How it impressed me: _____

_____

_____

_____

# MY READING HIGHLIGHTS

"Now, my children, listen to me. Those who follow my ways are happy. Listen to my teaching, and you will be wise.  Do not ignore it. Those who listen to me are happy. They stand watching at my door every day. They are at my open door waiting to be with me." —Proverbs 8:32-34 (NCV)

Translation _____ Year _____

☐ **Sunday** Date _____ All I read today _____

Best thing I marked today: *Reference* _____

*Thought:* _____

_____

How it impressed me: _____

_____

_____

_____

☐ **Monday** Date _____ All I read today _____

Best thing I marked today: *Reference* _____

*Thought:* _____

_____

How it impressed me: _____

_____

_____

_____

☐ **Tuesday** Date _____ All I read today _____

Best thing I marked today: *Reference* _____

*Thought:* _____

_____

How it impressed me: _____

_____

_____

☐ **Wednesday** Date_____ All I read today_____

Best thing I marked today: *Reference* _____

*Thought:* _____

How it impressed me: _____

☐ **Thursday** Date_____ All I read today_____

Best thing I marked today: *Reference* _____

*Thought:* _____

How it impressed me: _____

☐ **Friday** Date_____ All I read today_____

Best thing I marked today: *Reference* _____

*Thought:* _____

How it impressed me: _____

☐ **Saturday** Date_____ All I read today_____

Best thing I marked today: *Reference* _____

*Thought:* _____

How it impressed me: _____

# MY READING HIGHLIGHTS

"Now, my children, listen to me. Those who follow my ways are happy. Listen to my teaching, and you will be wise.  Do not ignore it. Those who listen to me are happy. They stand watching at my door every day. They are at my open door waiting to be with me." —Proverbs 8:32-34 (NCV)

Translation _____ Year _____

☐ **Sunday** Date _____ All I read today _____

Best thing I marked today: *Reference* _____

*Thought:* _____

_____

How it impressed me: _____

_____

_____

☐ **Monday** Date _____ All I read today _____

Best thing I marked today: *Reference* _____

*Thought:* _____

_____

How it impressed me: _____

_____

_____

_____

☐ **Tuesday** Date _____ All I read today _____

Best thing I marked today: *Reference* _____

*Thought:* _____

_____

How it impressed me: _____

_____

_____

□ **Wednesday** Date _____ All I read today _____

Best thing I marked today: *Reference* _____

*Thought:* _____

_____

How it impressed me: _____

_____

_____

_____

□ **Thursday** Date _____ All I read today _____

Best thing I marked today: *Reference* _____

*Thought:* _____

_____

How it impressed me: _____

_____

_____

_____

□ **Friday** Date _____ All I read today _____

Best thing I marked today: *Reference* _____

*Thought:* _____

_____

How it impressed me: _____

_____

_____

_____

□ **Saturday** Date _____ All I read today _____

Best thing I marked today: *Reference* _____

*Thought:* _____

_____

How it impressed me: _____

_____

_____

_____

# MY READING HIGHLIGHTS

"Now, my children, listen to me. Those who follow my ways are happy. Listen to my teaching, and you will be wise.  Do not ignore it. Those who listen to me are happy. They stand watching at my door every day. They are at my open door waiting to be with me." —Proverbs 8:32-34 (NCV)

Translation _____ Year _____

☐ **Sunday** Date _____ All I read today _____

Best thing I marked today: *Reference* _____

*Thought:* _____

_____

How it impressed me: _____

_____

_____

_____

☐ **Monday** Date _____ All I read today _____

Best thing I marked today: *Reference* _____

*Thought:* _____

_____

How it impressed me: _____

_____

_____

_____

☐ **Tuesday** Date _____ All I read today _____

Best thing I marked today: *Reference* _____

*Thought:* _____

_____

How it impressed me: _____

_____

_____

☐ **Wednesday** Date_____ All I read today _____

Best thing I marked today: *Reference* _____

*Thought:* _____

_____

How it impressed me: _____

_____

_____

_____

☐ **Thursday** Date_____ All I read today _____

Best thing I marked today: *Reference* _____

*Thought:* _____

_____

How it impressed me: _____

_____

_____

_____

☐ **Friday** Date_____ All I read today _____

Best thing I marked today: *Reference* _____

*Thought:* _____

_____

How it impressed me: _____

_____

_____

_____

☐ **Saturday** Date_____ All I read today _____

Best thing I marked today: *Reference* _____

*Thought:* _____

_____

How it impressed me: _____

_____

_____

_____

# MY READING HIGHLIGHTS

"Now, my children, listen to me. Those who follow my ways are happy. Listen to my teaching, and you will be wise. Do not ignore it. Those who listen to me are happy. They stand watching at my door every day. They are at my open door waiting to be with me." —Proverbs 8:32-34 (NCV)

Translation _____ Year _____

☐ **Sunday** Date _____ All I read today _____

Best thing I marked today: *Reference* _____

*Thought:* _____

_____

How it impressed me: _____

_____

_____

_____

☐ **Monday** Date _____ All I read today _____

Best thing I marked today: *Reference* _____

*Thought:* _____

_____

How it impressed me: _____

_____

_____

_____

☐ **Tuesday** Date _____ All I read today _____

Best thing I marked today: *Reference* _____

*Thought:* _____

_____

How it impressed me: _____

_____

_____

_____

☐ **Wednesday** Date_____ All I read today _____

Best thing I marked today: *Reference* _____

*Thought:* _____

_____

How it impressed me: _____

_____

_____

_____

☐ **Thursday** Date_____ All I read today _____

Best thing I marked today: *Reference* _____

*Thought:* _____

_____

How it impressed me: _____

_____

_____

_____

☐ **Friday** Date_____ All I read today _____

Best thing I marked today: *Reference* _____

*Thought:* _____

_____

How it impressed me: _____

_____

_____

_____

☐ **Saturday** Date_____ All I read today _____

Best thing I marked today: *Reference* _____

*Thought:* _____

_____

How it impressed me: _____

_____

_____

_____

# MY READING HIGHLIGHTS

"Now, my children, listen to me. Those who follow my ways are happy. Listen to my teaching, and you will be wise. Do not ignore it. Those who listen to me are happy. They stand watching at my door every day. They are at my open door waiting to be with me." —Proverbs 8:32-34 (NCV)

Translation _____ Year _____

☐ **Sunday** Date _____ All I read today _____

Best thing I marked today: *Reference* _____

*Thought:* _____

_____

How it impressed me: _____

_____

_____

☐ **Monday** Date _____ All I read today _____

Best thing I marked today: *Reference* _____

*Thought:* _____

_____

How it impressed me: _____

_____

_____

☐ **Tuesday** Date _____ All I read today _____

Best thing I marked today: *Reference* _____

*Thought:* _____

_____

How it impressed me: _____

_____

_____

☐ **Wednesday** Date_____ All I read today _____

Best thing I marked today: *Reference* _____

*Thought:* _____

How it impressed me: _____

☐ **Thursday** Date_____ All I read today _____

Best thing I marked today: *Reference* _____

*Thought:* _____

How it impressed me: _____

☐ **Friday** Date _____ All I read today _____

Best thing I marked today: *Reference* _____

*Thought:* _____

How it impressed me: _____

☐ **Saturday** Date _____ All I read today _____

Best thing I marked today: *Reference* _____

*Thought:* _____

How it impressed me: _____

# MY READING PROGRESS

**OLD TESTAMENT**

| Genesis | 1 | 2 | 3 | 4 | 5 | 6 | 7 | 8 | 9 | 10 | 11 | 12 | 13 | 14 | 15 | 16 | 17 | 18 | 19 | 20 | 21 |
|---|---|---|---|---|---|---|---|---|---|---|---|---|---|---|---|---|---|---|---|---|---|
| | 22 | 23 | 24 | 25 | 26 | 27 | 28 | 29 | 30 | 31 | 32 | 33 | 34 | 35 | 36 | 37 | 38 | 39 | 40 | 41 | 42 |
| | 43 | 44 | 45 | 46 | 47 | 48 | 49 | 50 | | | | | | | | | | | | | |
| Exodus | 1 | 2 | 3 | 4 | 5 | 6 | 7 | 8 | 9 | 10 | 11 | 12 | 13 | 14 | 15 | 16 | 17 | 18 | 19 | 20 | 21 |
| | 22 | 23 | 24 | 25 | 26 | 27 | 28 | 29 | 30 | 31 | 32 | 33 | 34 | 35 | 36 | 37 | 38 | 39 | 40 | | |
| Leviticus | 1 | 2 | 3 | 4 | 5 | 6 | 7 | 8 | 9 | 10 | 11 | 12 | 13 | 14 | 15 | 16 | 17 | 18 | 19 | 20 | 21 |
| | 22 | 23 | 24 | 25 | 26 | 27 | | | | | | | | | | | | | | | |
| Numbers | 1 | 2 | 3 | 4 | 5 | 6 | 7 | 8 | 9 | 10 | 11 | 12 | 13 | 14 | 15 | 16 | 17 | 18 | 19 | 20 | 21 |
| | 22 | 23 | 24 | 25 | 26 | 27 | 28 | 29 | 30 | 31 | 32 | 33 | 34 | 35 | 36 | | | | | | |
| Deut. | 1 | 2 | 3 | 4 | 5 | 6 | 7 | 8 | 9 | 10 | 11 | 12 | 13 | 14 | 15 | 16 | 17 | 18 | 19 | 20 | 21 |
| | 22 | 23 | 24 | 25 | 26 | 27 | 28 | 29 | 30 | 31 | 32 | 33 | 34 | | | | | | | | |
| Joshua | 1 | 2 | 3 | 4 | 5 | 6 | 7 | 8 | 9 | 10 | 11 | 12 | 13 | 14 | 15 | 16 | 17 | 18 | 19 | 20 | 21 |
| | 22 | 23 | 24 | | | | | | | | | | | | | | | | | | |
| Judges | 1 | 2 | 3 | 4 | 5 | 6 | 7 | 8 | 9 | 10 | 11 | 12 | 13 | 14 | 15 | 16 | 17 | 18 | 19 | 20 | 21 |
| Ruth | 1 | 2 | 3 | 4 | | | | | | | | | | | | | | | | | |
| 1 Samuel | 1 | 2 | 3 | 4 | 5 | 6 | 7 | 8 | 9 | 10 | 11 | 12 | 13 | 14 | 15 | 16 | 17 | 18 | 19 | 20 | 21 |
| | 22 | 23 | 24 | 25 | 26 | 27 | 28 | 29 | 30 | 31 | | | | | | | | | | | |
| 2 Samuel | 1 | 2 | 3 | 4 | 5 | 6 | 7 | 8 | 9 | 10 | 11 | 12 | 13 | 14 | 15 | 16 | 17 | 18 | 19 | 20 | 21 |
| | 22 | 23 | 24 | | | | | | | | | | | | | | | | | | |
| 1 Kings | 1 | 2 | 3 | 4 | 5 | 6 | 7 | 8 | 9 | 10 | 11 | 12 | 13 | 14 | 15 | 16 | 17 | 18 | 19 | 20 | 21 |
| | 22 | | | | | | | | | | | | | | | | | | | | |
| 2 Kings | 1 | 2 | 3 | 4 | 5 | 6 | 7 | 8 | 9 | 10 | 11 | 12 | 13 | 14 | 15 | 16 | 17 | 18 | 19 | 20 | 21 |
| | 22 | 23 | 24 | 25 | | | | | | | | | | | | | | | | | |
| 1 Chron. | 1 | 2 | 3 | 4 | 5 | 6 | 7 | 8 | 9 | 10 | 11 | 12 | 13 | 14 | 15 | 16 | 17 | 18 | 19 | 20 | 21 |
| | 22 | 23 | 24 | 25 | 26 | 27 | 28 | 29 | | | | | | | | | | | | | |
| 2 Chron. | 1 | 2 | 3 | 4 | 5 | 6 | 7 | 8 | 9 | 10 | 11 | 12 | 13 | 14 | 15 | 16 | 17 | 18 | 19 | 20 | 21 |
| | 22 | 23 | 24 | 25 | 26 | 27 | 28 | 29 | 30 | 31 | 32 | 33 | 34 | 35 | 36 | | | | | | |
| Ezra | 1 | 2 | 3 | 4 | 5 | 6 | 7 | 8 | 9 | 10 | | | | | | | | | | | |
| Nehemiah | 1 | 2 | 3 | 4 | 5 | 6 | 7 | 8 | 9 | 10 | 11 | 12 | 13 | | | | | | | | |
| Esther | 1 | 2 | 3 | 4 | 5 | 6 | 7 | 8 | 9 | 10 | | | | | | | | | | | |
| Job | 1 | 2 | 3 | 4 | 5 | 6 | 7 | 8 | 9 | 10 | 11 | 12 | 13 | 14 | 15 | 16 | 17 | 18 | 19 | 20 | 21 |
| | 22 | 23 | 24 | 25 | 26 | 27 | 28 | 29 | 30 | 31 | 32 | 33 | 34 | 35 | 36 | 37 | 38 | 39 | 40 | 41 | 42 |
| Psalms | 1 | 2 | 3 | 4 | 5 | 6 | 7 | 8 | 9 | 10 | 11 | 12 | 13 | 14 | 15 | 16 | 17 | 18 | 19 | 20 | 21 |
| | 22 | 23 | 24 | 25 | 26 | 27 | 28 | 29 | 30 | 31 | 32 | 33 | 34 | 35 | 36 | 37 | 38 | 39 | 40 | 41 | 42 |
| | 43 | 44 | 45 | 46 | 47 | 48 | 49 | 50 | 51 | 52 | 53 | 54 | 55 | 56 | 57 | 58 | 59 | 60 | 61 | 62 | 63 |
| | 64 | 65 | 66 | 67 | 68 | 69 | 70 | 71 | 72 | 73 | 74 | 75 | 76 | 77 | 78 | 79 | 80 | 81 | 82 | 83 | 84 |
| | 85 | 86 | 87 | 88 | 89 | 90 | 91 | 92 | 93 | 94 | 95 | 96 | 97 | 98 | 99 | 100 | 101 | 102 | 103 | 104 | 105 |
| | 106 | 107 | 108 | 109 | 110 | 111 | 112 | 113 | 114 | 115 | 116 | 117 | 118 | 119 | 120 | 121 | 122 | 123 | 124 | 125 | 126 |
| | 127 | 128 | 129 | 130 | 131 | 132 | 133 | 134 | 135 | 136 | 137 | 138 | 139 | 140 | 141 | 142 | 143 | 144 | 145 | 146 | 147 |
| | 148 | 149 | 150 | | | | | | | | | | | | | | | | | | |
| Proverbs | 1 | 2 | 3 | 4 | 5 | 6 | 7 | 8 | 9 | 10 | 11 | 12 | 13 | 14 | 15 | 16 | 17 | 18 | 19 | 20 | 21 |
| | 22 | 23 | 24 | 25 | 26 | 27 | 28 | 29 | 30 | 31 | | | | | | | | | | | |
| Ecclesiastes | 1 | 2 | 3 | 4 | 5 | 6 | 7 | 8 | 9 | 10 | 11 | 12 | | | | | | | | | |
| Song of Songs | 1 | 2 | 3 | 4 | 5 | 6 | 7 | 8 | | | | | | | | | | | | | |
| Isaiah | 1 | 2 | 3 | 4 | 5 | 6 | 7 | 8 | 9 | 10 | 11 | 12 | 13 | 14 | 15 | 16 | 17 | 18 | 19 | 20 | 21 |
| | 22 | 23 | 24 | 25 | 26 | 27 | 28 | 29 | 30 | 31 | 32 | 33 | 34 | 35 | 36 | 37 | 38 | 39 | 40 | 41 | 42 |
| | 43 | 44 | 45 | 46 | 47 | 48 | 49 | 50 | 51 | 52 | 53 | 54 | 55 | 56 | 57 | 58 | 59 | 60 | 61 | 62 | 63 |
| | 64 | 65 | 66 | | | | | | | | | | | | | | | | | | |

| Jeremiah | 1 | 2 | 3 | 4 | 5 | 6 | 7 | 8 | 9 | 10 | 11 | 12 | 13 | 14 | 15 | 16 | 17 | 18 | 19 | 20 | 21 |
|---|---|---|---|---|---|---|---|---|---|---|---|---|---|---|---|---|---|---|---|---|---|
| | 22 | 23 | 24 | 25 | 26 | 27 | 28 | 29 | 30 | 31 | 32 | 33 | 34 | 35 | 36 | 37 | 38 | 39 | 40 | 41 | 42 |
| | 43 | 44 | 45 | 46 | 47 | 48 | 49 | 50 | 51 | 52 | | | | | | | | | | | |
| Lam. | 1 | 2 | 3 | 4 | 5 | | | | | | | | | | | | | | | | |
| Ezekiel | 1 | 2 | 3 | 4 | 5 | 6 | 7 | 8 | 9 | 10 | 11 | 12 | 13 | 14 | 15 | 16 | 17 | 18 | 19 | 20 | 21 |
| | 22 | 23 | 24 | 25 | 26 | 27 | 28 | 29 | 30 | 31 | 32 | 33 | 34 | 35 | 36 | 37 | 38 | 39 | 40 | 41 | 42 |
| | 43 | 44 | 45 | 46 | 47 | 48 | | | | | | | | | | | | | | | |
| Daniel | 1 | 2 | 3 | 4 | 5 | 6 | 7 | 8 | 9 | 10 | 11 | 12 | | | | | | | | | |
| Hosea | 1 | 2 | 3 | 4 | 5 | 6 | 7 | 8 | 9 | 10 | 11 | 12 | 13 | 14 | | | | | | | |
| Joel | 1 | 2 | 3 | | | | | | | | | | | | | | | | | | |
| Amos | 1 | 2 | 3 | 4 | 5 | 6 | 7 | 8 | 9 | | | | | | | | | | | | |
| Obadiah | 1 | | | | | | | | | | | | | | | | | | | | |
| Jonah | 1 | 2 | 3 | 4 | | | | | | | | | | | | | | | | | |
| Micah | 1 | 2 | 3 | 4 | 5 | 6 | 7 | | | | | | | | | | | | | | |
| Nahum | 1 | 2 | 3 | | | | | | | | | | | | | | | | | | |
| Habakkuk | 1 | 2 | 3 | | | | | | | | | | | | | | | | | | |
| Zephaniah | 1 | 2 | 3 | | | | | | | | | | | | | | | | | | |
| Haggai | 1 | 2 | | | | | | | | | | | | | | | | | | | |
| Zechariah | 1 | 2 | 3 | 4 | 5 | 6 | 7 | 8 | 9 | 10 | 11 | 12 | 13 | 14 | | | | | | | |
| Malachi | 1 | 2 | 3 | 4 | | | | | | | | | | | | | | | | | |

## NEW TESTAMENT

| Matthew | 1 | 2 | 3 | 4 | 5 | 6 | 7 | 8 | 9 | 10 | 11 | 12 | 13 | 14 | 15 | 16 | 17 | 18 | 19 | 20 | 21 |
|---|---|---|---|---|---|---|---|---|---|---|---|---|---|---|---|---|---|---|---|---|---|
| | 22 | 23 | 24 | 25 | 26 | 27 | 28 | | | | | | | | | | | | | | |
| Mark | 1 | 2 | 3 | 4 | 5 | 6 | 7 | 8 | 9 | 10 | 11 | 12 | 13 | 14 | 15 | 16 | | | | | |
| Luke | 1 | 2 | 3 | 4 | 5 | 6 | 7 | 8 | 9 | 10 | 11 | 12 | 13 | 14 | 15 | 16 | 17 | 18 | 19 | 20 | 21 |
| | 22 | 23 | 24 | | | | | | | | | | | | | | | | | | |
| John | 1 | 2 | 3 | 4 | 5 | 6 | 7 | 8 | 9 | 10 | 11 | 12 | 13 | 14 | 15 | 16 | 17 | 18 | 19 | 20 | 21 |
| Acts | 1 | 2 | 3 | 4 | 5 | 6 | 7 | 8 | 9 | 10 | 11 | 12 | 13 | 14 | 15 | 16 | 17 | 18 | 19 | 20 | 21 |
| | 22 | 23 | 24 | 25 | 26 | 27 | 28 | | | | | | | | | | | | | | |
| Romans | 1 | 2 | 3 | 4 | 5 | 6 | 7 | 8 | 9 | 10 | 11 | 12 | 13 | 14 | 15 | 16 | | | | | |
| 1 Cor. | 1 | 2 | 3 | 4 | 5 | 6 | 7 | 8 | 9 | 10 | 11 | 12 | 13 | 14 | 15 | 16 | | | | | |
| 2 Cor. | 1 | 2 | 3 | 4 | 5 | 6 | 7 | 8 | 9 | 10 | 11 | 12 | 13 | | | | | | | | |
| Galatians | 1 | 2 | 3 | 4 | 5 | 6 | | | | | | | | | | | | | | | |
| Ephesians | 1 | 2 | 3 | 4 | 5 | 6 | | | | | | | | | | | | | | | |
| Philippians | 1 | 2 | 3 | 4 | | | | | | | | | | | | | | | | | |
| Colossians | 1 | 2 | 3 | 4 | | | | | | | | | | | | | | | | | |
| 1 Thess. | 1 | 2 | 3 | 4 | 5 | | | | | | | | | | | | | | | | |
| 2 Thess. | 1 | 2 | 3 | | | | | | | | | | | | | | | | | | |
| 1 Timothy | 1 | 2 | 3 | 4 | 5 | 6 | | | | | | | | | | | | | | | |
| 2 Timothy | 1 | 2 | 3 | 4 | | | | | | | | | | | | | | | | | |
| Titus | 1 | 2 | 3 | | | | | | | | | | | | | | | | | | |
| Philemon | 1 | | | | | | | | | | | | | | | | | | | | |
| Hebrews | 1 | 2 | 3 | 4 | 5 | 6 | 7 | 8 | 9 | 10 | 11 | 12 | 13 | | | | | | | | |
| James | 1 | 2 | 3 | 4 | 5 | | | | | | | | | | | | | | | | |
| 1 Peter | 1 | 2 | 3 | 4 | 5 | | | | | | | | | | | | | | | | |
| 2 Peter | 1 | 2 | 3 | | | | | | | | | | | | | | | | | | |
| 1 John | 1 | 2 | 3 | 4 | 5 | | | | | | | | | | | | | | | | |
| 2 John | 1 | | | | | | | | | | | | | | | | | | | | |
| 3 John | 1 | | | | | | | | | | | | | | | | | | | | |
| Jude | 1 | | | | | | | | | | | | | | | | | | | | |
| Revelation | 1 | 2 | 3 | 4 | 5 | 6 | 7 | 8 | 9 | 10 | 11 | 12 | 13 | 14 | 15 | 16 | 17 | 18 | 19 | 20 | 21 |
| | 22 | | | | | | | | | | | | | | | | | | | | |

# NOTES

1. UN Food and Agriculture Organization, "Undernourishment Around the World in 2010" in *The State of Food Insecurity in the World in 2010*, 8, http://www.fao.org/docrep/013/i1683e/i1683e.pdf.

2. William Barkley, *Jesus as They Saw Him* (New York: Harper and Row, 1962), quoted in The Navigators, *Design for Discipleship* (Colorado Springs, CO: NavPress, 1973), used by permission.

3. LeRoy Eims, *Winning Ways* (Wheaton, IL: Victor Books, 1980), 122.

4. M. J. Erickson, *The Concise Dictionary of Christian Theology* (Grand Rapids, MI: Baker, 1994).

NCM focuses on helping churches become more intentional in discipleship and outreach. NCM staff help pastors, church leaders, and lifelong laborers across the United States develop an effective and personalized approach to accomplishing the Great Commission.

NCM works alongside the local church to grow intentional disciplemaking cultures, as reflected in the following illustration:

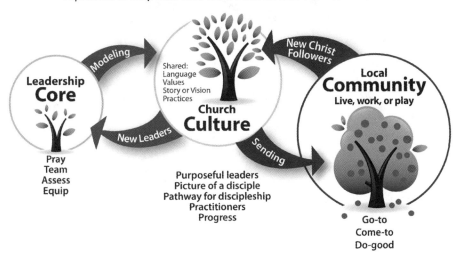

NCM also offers seminars, materials, and coaching to help the local church see discipleship flourish in successive generations. See our web page for further information on how NCM can help you.

www.navigators.org/ncm
or email to ncm@navigators.org
or call our NCM Office at (719) 594-2446
or write to PO Box 6000, Colorado Springs, CO 80934

# Continue to grow as part of God's family with the rest of **THE 2:7 SERIES.**

**Deepening Your Roots in God's Family**
The Navigators

The second book in THE 2:7 SERIES will teach you how to make Christ the Lord of your life. You'll discover how easy it is to branch out by reviewing your spiritual life and sharing it with others.

978-1-61521-638-3

**Bearing Fruit in God's Family**
The Navigators

By walking you through a simple yet effective approach to explaining the gospel to others, the third study in THE 2:7 SERIES will help you become a fruitful member of God's family.

978-1-61521-637-6

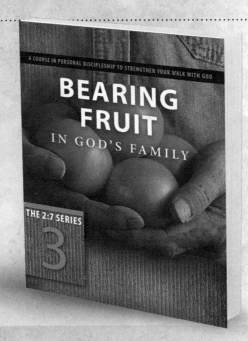